BEAUTY OF THE WILD

BEAUTY

of the

WILD

A LIFE DESIGNING LANDSCAPES

INSPIRED BY NATURE

DARREL MORRISON

LIBRARY OF AMERICAN LANDSCAPE HISTORY

AMHERST, MASSACHUSETTS

Library of American Landscape History
P.O. Box 1323
Amherst, MA 01004
www.lalh.org

Printed in the United States of America by Porter Print Group, LLC

Library of Congress Control Number: 2020947467
ISBN: 978-1-952620-28-7

Designed by Jonathan D. Lippincott
Set in Sabon

Distributed by
National Book Network
nbnbooks.com

Frontispiece:
Ox-eye (*Heliopsis helianthoides*) in mesic prairie section, Native Plant Garden, University of Wisconsin–Madison. Photograph by Robert Jaeger.

Chapter openers:
2: Sideoats grama (*Bouteloua curtipendula*) and prairie dropseed (*Sporobolus heterolepis*). Photograph by Susan Carpenter.
6: Whorled milkweed (*Asclepias verticillata*). Photograph by Susan Carpenter.
20: Prairie blue-eyed grass (*Sisyrinchium campestre*). Photograph by Susan Carpenter.
30: Prairie cinquefoil (*Potentilla arguta*) with big bluestem (*Andropogon gerardii*), white sage (*Artemisia ludoviciana*), and prairie coreopsis (*Coreopsis palmata*). Photograph by Susan Carpenter.
38: Nannyberry (*Viburnum lentago*). Photograph by Susan Carpenter.
68: Prairie cinquefoil (*Potentilla arguta*). Photograph by Susan Carpenter.
96: Ripened sideoats grama (*Boutelua curtipendula*) with silky aster (*Symphyotrichum sericeum*). Photograph by Susan Carpenter.
120: Paper birch (*Betula papyrifera*). Photograph by Susan Carpenter.
142: Wild bergamot (*Monarda fistulosa*). Photograph by Jonathan D. Lippincott.
152: Drummond's milkvetch (*Astragalus drummondii*). Photograph by Robin Karson.
164: Bird's-foot violet (*Viola pedata*). Photograph by Fritz Flohr Reynolds (CC BY-SA 3.0).

Storm King Art Center sculpture credits appear on page 184.

Publication of this book was aided by a generous grant from Furthermore: a program of the J. M. Kaplan Fund

For

Margaret and Jon

Nomita and Scott

CONTENTS

Prologue: Wheatfield under Thunderclouds   3

1. Iowa Farm   7

2. Out of the Nest   21

3. Early Forays in Design   31

4. Merging Ecology with Design   39

5. Southern Odyssey   69

6. Expanding Horizons   97

7. New York City Decade   121

8. Restoring the Beauty of the Wild   143

9. Under a Montana Sky   153

Epilogue: Back to the Prairie   165

Notes   169

Acknowledgments   173

Index   177

BEAUTY OF THE WILD

PROLOGUE: WHEATFIELD UNDER THUNDERCLOUDS

Making my way through the galleries of the Van Gogh Museum in Amsterdam a decade ago, I basked in the abundance of two hundred of Vincent van Gogh's bold-stroke paintings—sunflowers, irises, cypresses, black ravens hovering over golden fields. Then I came upon *Wheatfield under Thunderclouds,* painted in Auvers-sur-Oise, France, in July 1890, just days before the artist died. I stopped short and gazed at the painting, with its deep cobalt sky and roiling storm clouds over a patchwork of gently sloping fields stretching to the horizon. I had seen that sky and those thunderheads before. I remembered feeling excitement mixed with trepidation as thunderstorms approached from the west on hot, humid summer afternoons over fields of corn, soybeans, oats, alfalfa, and clover. I was transported back to the farm in southwest Iowa where I grew up many years ago.

A windbreak of silver maples and Siberian elms wrapped around the west and north sides of the farmstead. To see the full panoramic view of approaching storms, I had to leave the cluster of buildings and go beyond the windbreak. I ran barefoot, past the trees, at the first flashes of lightning and distant rumble of the approaching storm. After reaching a good vantage point, I watched the lightning become silver streaks piercing the dark blue sky and heard the rolling thunder become sharp claps, ever closer. The first big drops released the unforgettable smell of rain on dust. As the wind picked up, tossing the tree

Wildflowers in bloom, Kalsow Prairie State Preserve, Manson, IA. Photograph by Tom Bean.

branches in the windbreak, I raced back to take cover in the barn. Inside, lying in the hay, I listened to the wind whipping the rain into sheets pounding on the tin roof, punctuated by the pelting of hailstones. After a time, the storm's histrionics subsided, the wind and the thunder tapered off, and the rain became calmer and steadier. When the rain stopped, I ventured out beyond the windbreak once more, feeling the wet earth under my bare feet and watching the late afternoon sun break through the clouds, lighting an iridescent wet landscape with an increasingly golden light. A western meadowlark perched on a fence post, celebrating the rain and the sun with its mellifluous song.

That farm in southwestern Iowa is the first place I can remember. We referred to it as "our place" and not as "our farm." Our neighbors' farms were "the Mitchell place," "the McBride place," and "the Strong place." Our place was the first of many places that shaped my life and my work as a designer of landscapes.

1

IOWA FARM

On a hot summer afternoon, June 20, 1937, I was born on a farm rented by my parents, Rosy and Raymond, a mile and a half east of Orient, Iowa, in the southwestern part of the state. My brothers, five-year-old Kenneth and two-year-old Eldon, were there to greet me. A few months later, my mother and father made the momentous decision to buy the only farm they ever owned, their home for the next four decades. "Our place" was two miles west and a mile and a half north of Orient on State Highway 25. Directions in Iowa were always expressed in terms of the one-mile, north-south, east-west grid laid over the state's flat to rolling topography during the initial land survey, begun in the 1830s. Our place was a quarter section, or 160 acres. The grid was manifested visually by straight east-west and north-south county roads every mile. Within each of those square-mile sections, there were typically four farmsteads, usually with a rectilinear windbreak on the north and west sides of the cluster of buildings—the house, barns, and sheds.

Before the square-mile grid was established, 85 percent of the area that became the state of Iowa in 1846 had been covered by tallgrass prairie—30 million acres of it. Our place was at the heart of a vast 640-million-acre mid-continent prairie where there had been a human presence for 12,000 years. When European explorers arrived in the early nineteenth century, they often described this nearly treeless landscape, with its waves of dominant grasses, as

(*Top*) Darrel, age 5, with Mickey and cats; (*bottom*) Darrel, age 1, with parents Rosy and Raymond and brothers Kenneth (*left*) and Eldon on the Iowa farm.

The Southern Wildlands, Clarke, Madison, and Warren Counties, IA. Photograph courtesy Iowa Natural Heritage Foundation.

an inland sea. Big bluestem, little bluestem, Indiangrass, switchgrass, northern prairie cordgrass, prairie dropseed, and needlegrass accounted for 90 percent of the biomass in the prairie. Dozens of species of "forbs," broadleaf flowering plants—butterfly weed, prairie phlox, spiderwort, shooting star, puccoon, bergamot, pale purple coneflower, sunflowers, goldenrods, and asters, among them—drifted through the grasses, an ever-changing impressionistic blanket of color over the land.

A combination of climatic factors and fires—both lightning-caused fires and those set by the Native American populations—had kept the prairie in a nearly treeless state for a hundred centuries. One exception was the bur oak, with its thick bark and drought tolerance, and it persisted in the prairie as scattered individuals and in small groves. Initially, early settlers from Europe and the eastern United States were skeptical of land that didn't produce "timber." They soon recognized that the deep topsoil built up by prairie plants over ten thousand years was potentially some of the richest farmland in the world. But the dense, fibrous root system of prairie plants, extending down as much as fifteen feet, made it nearly impossible to break the prairie sod with the wood bottom plows of the early nineteenth century. Everything changed in 1837—one hundred years before I was born—when John Deere invented a steel bottom plow capable of breaking the tough prairie sod. Within a surprisingly short period of only two or three decades, prairie vegetation disappeared from vast areas. It has been estimated that 99.9 percent of Iowa's prairie was plowed under. The sea of native grasses waving in the nearly constant wind

Boundary between tallgrass prairie preserve and soybean field, Manson, IA. Photograph by Tom Bean.

was replaced by a patchwork of imported species: wheat, corn, oats, red clover, sweet clover, alfalfa, and soybeans.

In the 1940s, the landscape of the rolling hills on our place was inhabited by an almost totally different set of species from those of the previous centuries, yet certain aspects of the prairie remained unchanged. Once I got beyond the protective windbreak, there was the wind. I especially loved the warm, moist spring winds hitting my skin. And there was still the largely unbroken sky, with its ever-changing moods: fluffy white cumulus clouds floating above on clear June days, their shadows moving over the rolling fields. There were the ominous cobalt clouds on steamy summer afternoons portending a thunderstorm and the leaden skies before January blizzards, depositing deep snow whipped by the wind into beautiful dunelike drifts.

When I was growing up, there were two holdouts on our place where native prairie species remained. One was a half-acre wet slough adjacent to the "crick," the small stream that cut through the middle of the farm. Dad had purposely saved this area, not putting drain tiles in it, because the slough grass, or northern prairie cordgrass, made a good water-repellant topping for hay. The cordgrass had another less-than-flattering name—ripgut grass— from the sharp, sawtooth edges of its six-foot arching leaves. It clearly earned its "ripgut" designation, and we wore protective clothing whenever we cut and pitched it to the tops of haystacks. The other refuge for native plants was in the right-of-way of State Highway 25, the east boundary of the farm. As a young child, I discovered delicately fragrant prairie roses there, along with beebalm, yellow coneflowers, and pale purple coneflowers. I often picked bouquets for my mother, who placed them in Mason jars as centerpieces for our kitchen table.

Daily life on the farm seemed unexceptional at the time. We lived in an 1880s wood frame house with sloping floors and ill-fitting windows. Electricity arrived when I was four. We were without running water or indoor plumbing until we built a new four-bedroom house in 1949. Before then, we hand-pumped water at the well and carried it in buckets for cooking, cleaning, clothes-washing, and Saturday night baths in a tub next to the wood-burning cookstove in the kitchen. We had an outhouse. I didn't think of us as being deprived. It was the way that we and our neighbors lived.

The large family garden—at least an acre of rich black Iowa soil near the

Waterman-Tuttle Tract, Waterman Prairie Wildlife Management Area, Cherokee County, IA. Photograph by Bruce Morrison.

house—was planted with a variety of vegetables and annual flowers. From the time we were five or six, my two older brothers and I were each assigned our own ten-by-ten-foot plot within the big garden. My first little garden began with neat rows of fast-growing, quickly rewarding vegetables like lettuces, radishes, and peas. Soon I felt the urge to embellish it, planting circles and squares of vegetables bordered with purple or white alyssum and dwarf marigolds and zinnias. As I got a little older, I began to help plant and weed the vegetable garden, which included a good representation of showy flowers: full-sized marigolds, zinnias, gladioli, cosmos, and cleomes.

Our meals were dominated by food we had grown and raised. Dinner, the noon meal on the farm, featured fried chicken, pork chops, roast beef, or ham, with mashed potatoes and gravy. In summer, there were freshly picked peas, lima beans, green beans, sweet corn, and sliced tomatoes, and, in winter, canned versions of these that Mom had put up the previous summer. Desserts were sour

Tallgrass prairie vegetation, Effigy Mounds National Monument, IA. Photograph by Tom Bean.

cream chocolate cake, cherry, apple, peach, or rhubarb pie, or various cobblers or upside-down cakes. Supper, in the evening after the farm chores were done, was leftovers from dinner or maybe sloppy joes or burgers. A frequent—and favorite—Sunday night supper consisted of grilled cheese sandwiches with Campbell's tomato soup. The five of us gathered around the kitchen table for meals three times a day, seven days a week, except on Sunday noon, when we often had various aunts, uncles, grandparents, and cousins for dinner after church. Then we added one, two, or three boards to the dining room table and set it with the good dishes—the china with the pale pink roses on the border. All twelve place settings are still in my cupboard seventy years later.

After supper during the school years, we boys sat at the dining room table next to the wood-burning heater, with homework laid out in front of us. Dad read the day's *Des Moines Tribune*, and Mom mended clothes, embroidered, or read from the current selection of the Book-of-the-Month Club. In those days, we listened to a regular lineup of radio shows on the Zenith radio: *Fibber McGee and Molly, The Great Gildersleeve, Truth or*

Darrel planting green beans in the big vegetable garden on the farm.

Consequences, The Shadow, and Groucho Marx's *You Bet Your Life*. There were always games to be played: checkers, Chinese checkers, and extended rounds of Monopoly. Dad wouldn't allow us to play cards (the ones with clubs, diamonds, spades, and hearts) because it might lead us down the path toward gambling, but Flinch and Touring were deemed safe. Often, someone would pop a dishpan of popcorn, well-buttered, that we ate during the radio shows or games. Popcorn is still my favorite wintertime snack, probably because it takes me back to those harmonious family nights around the dining room table.

They were not always harmonious, of course. We had our share of spats and teasing among three brothers. Being the youngest and smallest, I could complain that my older brothers were picking on me and get the hoped-for response from my parents, but there were also disadvantages to my position. One of these was growing up wearing mostly hand-me-down clothes, not just secondhand but thirdhand. Admittedly, I did get some new shirts, bib overalls, and jeans from J. C. Penney's at the beginning of each school year. When they became too tattered to wear to school, they were worn for farm chores.

Sunday clothes were different because they didn't wear out before they were outgrown. "The Saga of the Plaid Sport Coat" began when I was eight years old, in the third grade at Orient Consolidated School. One Saturday, we piled into the 1941 dark green Chevy on a shopping trip to Robert Hall's in Des Moines, where Mom and Dad bought us identical plaid sport coats, except for the size, of course. The three stairstep boys in matching sport coats with dark pants made a cute photograph. I wore my first coat until I was ten. By then, Eldon, now twelve, was outgrowing his at about the same rate, so it was automatically passed along to me. Meanwhile, Eldon could wear Kenneth's coat for the next two years. The cycle (or recycle) continued, and when I reached age twelve, I became the not-so-proud owner of Kenneth's plaid sport coat. Midway through my two-year term in the third coat, Mom and Dad took pity on me and we went back to Robert Hall's. I selected a dark green corduroy coat, a bit like velvet, without a hint of plaid.

An essential ritual on the farm was doing the chores, morning and evening, year-round. The livestock needed to be fed, the hens' eggs gathered, and the dairy cows milked, by hand, twice a day. Each of us had our own designated livestock to look after. I gravitated toward working with the herd

Darrel at the wheel with Kenneth (*left*) and Eldon on the Allis Chalmers tractor at the farm.

of seven cows, but we all shared the milking duties. In retrospect milking was an exercise in meditation—leaning against Sally's or Suzie's side, pull and squeeze, pull and squeeze hardly required thinking. My favorite chore connected with the dairy herd was getting the cows, herding them from the pasture to the barn during the warm months, to be milked morning and evening.

A part of the milking ritual was pouring very fresh warm milk into a couple of pans for the cats who gathered in the barn. The collection of cats varied dramatically, but there was a core group that we came to know very well: Fluffy, Sukey, Tiger, Ginger, Pansy, and Arnold. These were hard-working farm cats who earned their keep as mousers, reducing the mouse population in the granary and hay barn. Then there was Mickey, a small, short-haired dog, white with a few black spots, appropriately called a rat terrier. He had a deeply ingrained hatred of rats and happily kept their numbers in check.

When I was eleven, I undertook the writing and "publishing" of "The Cat Press," a biweekly, handwritten, three-column newspaper with a circulation of one. It came out every other Thursday morning, and meeting my self-imposed deadline often required late Wednesday nights. The news revolved around births and deaths (of which there were many), cats' hunting achievements, and their various antics. There was an annual "Most Popular Cat" contest in which my family cast votes for their favorites, as well as a "Cat of the Week" series featuring character sketches of our feline family. During slow news periods, I recorded the weights of each cat. "The Cat Press" had a four-year run, from 1948 to 1952, and my mother saved every issue.

From junior high through high school, I became the self-appointed garden designer of the flower beds and borders near the house. I took my assignment seriously, poring over the new Burpee's seed catalog when it arrived in the mail each January. Long winter evenings were spent pondering the year's order for seeds and bulbs. For several summers, I planted a tropical-looking bed around the chicken pen near the house consisting of a half circle of gigantic castor beans, which thrived on the soil enrichment that spilled through the fence. Surrounding the castor beans was a semicircular row of scarlet and yellow cannas and, in front of them, a row of scarlet sage. Subtlety never entered into the equation. Then there was a four-foot-wide border along the hot, west-facing wall of the house, which changed from year to year and included one particularly memorable planting of Royal Purple petunias bordered with Burpee's Yellow Pygmy marigolds.

The original lawn surrounding the 1880s house was a modest patch of Kentucky bluegrass. My brothers and I took turns mowing it with a push mower. Between that small plot of turf surrounding the old house and Highway 25 was at least an acre of rough forage grasses: orchard grass and timothy. Dad mowed it with a tractor-drawn sickle mower several times a year. But with the upgrade into the new four-bedroom house, it seemed only fitting that the setting should undergo an equivalent improvement. The rough grasses were cut short in the area to become lawn, and Dad broadcast a Kentucky bluegrass and fescue seed mix into it, using a hand-cranked broadcast seeder. Soon there was a uniform, mowable lawn that required a gasoline-powered mower. Mowing provided great exercise for my brothers and me, but we soon found it too tedious just to mow in straight back-and-forth rows. To reduce our boredom, we turned the task into an art form. Initially we mowed in north-south rows one week, east-west rows the next week, and diagonally the next. From there, we progressed to more fluid forms, mowing the first swath as a sweeping curve, or series of curves, in the middle of the lawn and working out from that beginning in each direction.

During the summer I turned fourteen, I decided to try my hand at a smaller-scale horticultural art form. Much to Dad's chagrin, I entered several arrangements in the Adair County Fair flower-arranging contest. My competition was mostly ladies in the garden club. Undaunted, I put together compositions of corn tassels, stalks of golden ripened oats, and purple-flowering alfalfa from the hayfield, in combination with traditional garden flowers. These "exuberant" arrangements were big winners in the eyes of the jury and even made the front page of the weekly *Adair County Free Press*. Dad read the story, but never said a word about it to me.

Both my parents expanded our horizons in many ways that were atypical for Iowa farm boys of my generation. When I was eight years old, they surprised us by having a new, upright Gulbransen piano delivered to the old farmhouse. I took piano lessons through high school and developed a lifelong love of music. During my teenage years, there were annual trips to the recently built Des Moines Art Center, designed by Eliel Saarinen. Through these visits, we were introduced to abstract expressionism and other modern art movements in Saarinen's sun-drenched galleries, with views out to *Man and Pegasus*, a striking Carl Milles sculpture in the central courtyard's reflecting pool. At the end of the afternoon, we returned to the farm and went about the evening chores. I remember milking Suzie or Sally, my mind filled with visions of the art we had seen that day.

The trips to the Des Moines Art Center influenced my brothers as well, though at that time none of us foresaw the impact art or design would have on our lives. After graduating from high school in 1951, Kenneth enrolled in the Kansas City Art Institute and subsequently became a commercial artist in a Minneapolis advertising agency. Eldon graduated from Iowa State College with an architectural degree in 1960 and established his own office in White Bear Lake, Minnesota. As a junior in high school, I first learned there was a professional field that merged art and design with the world of plants. My mother's brother, Raymond Mensing, had married Louise Kellenberg, and her brother graduated from Iowa State in landscape architecture. When I met Richard Kellenberg he was working in the venerable Kansas City, Missouri, landscape architecture firm of Hare & Hare, where he had a long and successful career. I was intrigued by the possibility of designing landscapes and gardens as a profession, especially because it was something I had done for pleasure on the farm.

By the spring of 1955, it was a foregone conclusion that in the fall I would attend Iowa State College, where I had been accepted for admission and granted a full in-state tuition scholarship for my freshman year. My course of study was less certain. After four years of publishing "The Cat Press," I continued to enjoy writing. My English teacher, Maude Rust, had introduced me to great literature, assigning weekly essays and encouraging the reading of Shakespeare. As a senior, I edited our school newspaper, *The Howl,* and considered majoring in journalism.

That May, my parents and I drove the hundred miles to Ames to attend Iowa State's annual student-run festival, VEISHEA (the acronym for the institution's five colleges: Veterinary Medicine, Engineering, Industrial Science, Home Economics, and Agriculture). Eldon joined us at the big VEISHEA parade, with its dozens of elaborate floats and multiple marching bands. Later, we went to the landscape architecture open house in a charming 1901 half-timber horse stable that had been renovated and repurposed as faculty offices, classrooms, and landscape design studios. We met John R. Fitzsimmons, head of the department, A. Maurice Hanson, Ralph R. Rothacker, and other faculty members who made us feel welcome and comfortable about my future. I was impressed by the student projects for estates, shopping centers, and school grounds rendered in pastels and even watercolors. The real showstopper, though, was the garden with brick paving and walls and a cascading pool surrounded by potted plants right there in a central studio space. It had a decidedly California feel about it, similar to gardens I later saw in *Sunset* magazine. Back at the farm, while milking the cows that evening and recalling the beautiful drawings and the lush garden, I chose my major.

The summer of 1955 was a full one: I continued to look after the flower borders, to mow the expanded lawn, and to get the cows morning and evening. I worked as a corn de-tassler for three weeks for the Pioneer Seed Corn Company and was paid by neighbors to walk their soybean fields and chop down any cockleburs or Canada thistles in the rows. I hoisted clover and alfalfa hay bales onto hay wagons. For the first time, I was an only child and felt a new closeness with Mom and Dad. I especially remember the evenings after supper at the end of a long day's work. The three of us sat in the wooden lawn chairs that my brothers and I had made in high school shop class, overlooking the garden, watching fireflies flitting through.

2

OUT OF THE NEST

At the end of the idyllic summer of 1955, I loaded my clothes into the Chevy and rode with Eldon to Ames. We rented rooms in Mrs. Wilcox's boarding house and shared a small kitchen with a third renter. My daily life at Iowa State involved walking from the house through the heart of campus, a flat to gently sloping open lawn framed by clusters of mature trees, many deciduous, but with groups of white pines in places. A broad, straight walkway crossed the space from Beardshear Hall, the columned central administration building, to Curtiss Hall, the central Agriculture College building. The landscape architecture building was on the eastern edge of campus. At this early point in my education, I wasn't aware of the careful thought and skillful design that went into such a planned landscape, but I genuinely appreciated the beauty of the calm, pastoral scene.

In A. Maurice Hanson's landscape architecture history class, I learned that the Olmsted firm and the Chicago-based designer O. C. Simonds had contributed to the campus design in the early twentieth century. In 1906, Olmsted Brothers wrote a report to the college president anticipating the college's rapid expansion and offering advice on appropriate methods of planning for future buildings and open spaces.[1] Beginning in the 1920s, one of my professors, Ralph Rothacker, worked as part of a team of landscape architects and planners on the campus expansion plan.[2]

During my first semester, as I made the adjustment to college life, Alvin Edgar's music appreciation class became a highlight of each week. In the wonderful semicircular Morrill Hall auditorium, with its curving balcony and excellent acoustics, Professor Edgar introduced us to a whole new world of music—from Gregorian chant to medieval, Renaissance, and Romantic. When he played *The Moldau* by Bedřich Smetana, I was transported by the composer's portrayal of the Moldau (or Vltava) River in (then) Czechoslovakia, as it grew from a trickling stream to a broad sweeping river, with a folk dance and a tumultuous thunderstorm along the way. I can still picture it, as if for the first time, and with the same powerful emotion. Professor Edgar also brought world-class musicians to perform on campus. As a freshman, I heard my first symphony orchestra concert. When the St. Louis Symphony started its program with the Prelude to Act I of Wagner's *Lohengrin,* I felt that I had never heard anything as beautiful as the string section's ethereal strains. While an undergraduate at Iowa State, I heard my first operas, the Boris Goldovsky Opera Company's renditions of Donizetti's *Don Pasquale* and Verdi's *La Traviata,* and then as a senior, the Japanese Kabuki theater, thanks to Dr. Edgar's efforts.

Among the required courses in my undergraduate degree program were several taught in the architecture department of the College of Engineering. The most inspiring of these was Basic Design taught by Clair Watson. His lectures took the form of "design chats," during which he would sit on a drafting stool or on the edge of a desk at the front of the room, without notes, talking insightfully about such things as the effects of lighting, color, and color combinations, or texture, with slides of artworks, textiles, interiors, and buildings to illustrate them. The architecture department also offered freehand drawing and painting classes, in which we used pens, Conté crayons, pastels, and watercolors. It felt good to be practicing a bit of "fine art" and to use our skills in the abstract design projects assigned by Professor Watson. I was not surprised when, in 1959, the year that I graduated, he was given one of the university's five Professor of the Year awards.

Meanwhile, the courses we took in the landscape architecture department comprised a solid, traditional program: landscape architecture history, technology (earthwork/grading and construction detailing), design studios, and the plant-related courses (plant materials and planting design). Even then, I didn't like the term "plant materials" with its implication that plants are some-

Morrison's graduation picture,
Iowa State College, 1959.

how equivalent to unchanging building materials, rather than living, growing beings. My favorite courses were the landscape design studios, which involved creating our own designs through a process of successive tracing paper sketches over base maps with the givens: buildings, streets/roads, topography, and existing vegetation. We experimented with design concepts and forms in plan view, modifying and refining our schemes with each successive layer. Those late nights provided opportunities to bond and to learn from each other by discussing our designs and graphic presentation techniques. At some point, we had to commit to a final design, and like students everywhere, I put that off as long as possible. Somehow, I would always meet the deadline but only barely, after several into-the-night sessions in the studio.

I will never forget the wonderful feeling of at last reaching the point of rendering a final drawing with colored pencils, chalk pastels, or, on rare occasions, watercolors on stretched watercolor paper. To this day, I find the coloring phase to be one of the most satisfying steps in the process, with the prospect of blending colors, overlaying colors, and selectively highlighting or fading out the intensity of color. I also liked the process of making grading plans. Early on, I came to appreciate topographic base maps, often with beautiful, fluid topographic lines, and I tried to emulate this fluidity in my plans.

The courses labeled "Plant Materials" involved memorizing characteristics of several hundred species of trees, shrubs, and vines included in Donald Wyman's books *Shrubs and Vines for American Gardens* (1949) and *Trees for American Gardens* (1951). Wyman was head of horticulture at Harvard University's Arnold Arboretum from 1935 to 1970, and his books fascinated me with their wealth of useful information—not only details like the location of each plant's origin, its hardiness zone, mature height, and blooming time but also foliage, with a special emphasis on fall color. We were introduced to a limited array of groundcovers such as English ivy and periwinkle, with the implication that they would generally be used as single-species "blankets," primarily in shaded areas. There was a seemingly unquestioned expectation that sunny areas would be planted with cool-season turfgrasses, Kentucky bluegrass being the primary species in lawn mixes.

Over the decades, many of the trees, shrubs, vines, and groundcovers in Wyman's books had been planted on the Iowa State campus, and in plant material classes with Professor Rothacker, we had the opportunity to see them up close. Exams in the class consisted of returning to the field, where he would point to a plant, and we would each write its Latin and common names on our exam sheet. In some cases, I must admit that I memorized the location of the plant on campus rather than the fine points of its physical characteristics, though many plant names were learned in the process.

During the spring of my final semester at Iowa State, Eldridge Lovelace, senior partner in the planning and landscape architecture firm Harland Bartholomew & Associates of St. Louis, came to the department to interview candidates for entry-level positions in the firm.[3] I interviewed, was offered a job, and accepted it, effective immediately upon graduation. In those days, new graduates rarely took a year off, or even a month, to travel or to "find themselves." I picked up my diploma on a Saturday morning and was at the farm that evening, milking Suzie and Sally. On Sunday morning, Eldon drove me to St. Louis. That afternoon, upon arriving in the city, I found a third-floor, non-air-conditioned room, just off Delmar Boulevard.

On Monday morning, Eldon headed back to Iowa and I took the bus downtown for my first day at Harland Bartholomew & Associates.[4] My work that summer consisted mostly of preparing land use maps, both existing and proposed land use for the firm's comprehensive plans of cities and counties throughout the Midwest. I spent numerous hours laying sheets of Zip-a-Tone patterns over base maps, sticky-side-down, and using an X-Acto knife to cut them precisely to match the various land use zones without piercing the underlying map. It was a bit like surgery, with much lower stakes. I always hoped to do a planting plan, but those were all assigned to Claire Avis, the chief designer.[5]

The highlight of the summer of 1959 was my first trip to New York City. Eldridge Lovelace, who was my supervisor, asked me to attend the annual meeting of the ASLA and to write summaries of selected talks. He incorporated these into his report on the meeting, later published in *Landscape Architecture Quarterly,* forerunner of *Landscape Architecture Magazine.* During the bus ride from LaGuardia Airport to my hotel, we passed cemeteries crowded with vertical tombstones—miniature versions of the skyscrapers emerging from the fog and smog of Manhattan. The conference was held at the Waldorf Astoria Hotel. I stayed at the Prince Albert (or was it the Prince Edward?) in the heart of Times Square, with all those bright lights right outside my window and more yellow cabs in one place than I had seen in my entire life.

When I was not at the ASLA presentations, feverishly taking notes, I played New York tourist, hitting many of the high spots (literally): the Top of the Rock Observation Deck at Rockefeller Center; the Empire State Building; the Cloisters in Washington Heights; the Great Lawn in Central Park; the overwhelming Metropolitan Museum. I bought a ticket to the final banquet of the convention at the Waldorf Astoria but ate most of my meals at the Times Square Howard Johnson's, Tad's Steakhouse on Seventh Avenue, with its striking plush red wallpaper, and the Horn & Hardart Automat, a brave new world for me.

It was beastly hot in St. Louis that summer. I escaped from my third-floor room some evenings by attending the current Broadway musical at the Municipal Opera, or "Muny," an 11,000-seat amphitheater set in the woods of Swope Park. Arriving at the amphitheater was always a bit of an event. As I made my way along the broad, curving walk, to the accompaniment of people chattering and a chorus of cicadas, I felt lonely, having only recently been separated from my three best friends in my landscape architecture class and my brother. It came as a relief when, at the end of the summer, HB&A assigned me to a field location closer to home, in Lincoln, Nebraska.

Life picked up for me when I rented a second-floor efficiency apartment in that city. Each work day, I walked from A Street northward past the State

Capitol building and on to the office in City Hall on O Street. Robert Cole Simonds was my immediate supervisor in Lincoln, where the firm had a contract to develop a comprehensive plan for the city and Lancaster County.[6] As the junior member of the office, I worked on a block-by-block land use survey, walking most of the streets of Lincoln and categorizing each lot as single-family residential, multiple-family residential, commercial, institutional, or industrial and drawing base maps and coloring or Zip-a-Toning them.

During my year in Lincoln, I made the hundred-mile trip home about a half dozen times, traveling aboard the Burlington Zephyr. In January, much of that trip was after dark. Sitting in a dim Vista-Dome car, I watched the flat, horizontal, snow-covered landscape speed by. Since then, I have ridden on night trains throughout the world, but that trip stands out most vividly in my memory. It was, I think, because this landscape of eastern Nebraska gave new meaning to the term "the plains," and in the bluish light of a full moon, I understood how dramatic and powerful a flat landscape can be.

One day in July 1960, I opened my mailbox in Lincoln and found a letter from the Adair County, Iowa, Selective Service office. I had expected my draft number to come up any day. After passing the required physical exam, I prepared to leave for Fort Des Moines on September 6. I hated the concept of joining the military but, being an obedient farm boy, never considered objecting to the summons. This was in the post-Korean, pre–Vietnam War period, and it was impossible to know where I might end up. Before departing, I visited my parents on the farm and was moved by my father's tears, one of the few times he ever cried in my presence.

My tour of duty began with basic training at Fort Hood, Texas, in the Second Armored Division, whose motto was "Hell on Wheels." For me, the eight weeks of training definitely corresponded with "hell": doing push-ups at midday on the asphalt parking lot outside the barracks under the broiling September sun; disassembling, cleaning, and reassembling my M1 rifle; bayonet practice; rifle range exercises; and endlessly polishing boots. Exhausted at the end of the day, I would fall into my bunk, dreading the drill sergeant's rude awakening at five the next morning, yelling at us to get in formation for calisthenics in the parking lot, still hot from the previous day's sun. But there were positive aspects of the time I spent deep in the heart of Texas. One was getting to know men from different races and backgrounds, as we lived and worked together.

The Texas landscape was an almost totally new world for me. The "landscaped" areas around our barracks and other buildings were essentially characterless expanses of parched lawns with clipped shrubs and scattered trees. But when we left the confines of these areas and got out into the field, there were remnants of a wilder native landscape, albeit in a battered state. I remember these remnants as generally dusty and flat, with muted colors, and years later realized I had probably been seeing drought-tolerant grama grasses, muhly, and buffalo grass, with flecks of the purple of dotted blazing star and the yellow of dyer's-weed goldenrod growing among them.

The culmination of the eight weeks of basic training was a five-day bivouac in this relatively untamed landscape, where we set up our pup tents and field kitchen to simulate a battlefield situation. The infamous night infiltration course required crawling on the ground while tracers fired just above our heads. But there were interludes, when bits of the "real" Texas revealed themselves. One evening, as we sat outside our tents eating our C-rations, I recognized sagebrush and prickly pear cactus (from my knowledge of John Wayne

Prickly pear cactus in Texas. Photograph by Darrel Morrison.

movies filmed in Monument Valley, Utah), as well as fine-textured grasses and diminutive flowering plants that brought an element of delicate beauty into the "war zone." I remember wanting to sketch these plants with a field guide in hand, rather than wielding my M1 rifle and bayonet over my shoulder, my pockets bulging with hand grenades.

In the end, I successfully graduated from basic training and was put on a train. I awoke the next morning as we arrived at Union Station in Washington, DC. Before my next train, I went out the front entrance to see the dome of the US Capitol, framed by the backlit leaves of sugar maples all aglow in the gold and orange foliage of early November. After a two-hour introduction to Washington, I returned to my assigned gate to board a local train, headed to another unknown destination. In Accotink, Virginia, an open army truck awaited me and a dozen or so other new soldiers with duffle bags. We climbed into the back and were taken to Fort Belvoir ("beautiful to behold"), Virginia, my home for the next twenty-two months.

Most likely because of my landscape architecture degree, I was assigned to the Thirtieth Engineering Battalion, a topographic mapmaking unit, where I became the battalion commander's administrative assistant. My duties included filing memos and army directives, making strong coffee, typing correspondence for the officers, and putting out the "Daily Bulletin," Monday through Friday. Most of the material for the bulletin was handed down from higher levels and left little room for creative writing. The battalion commander was a barrel-chested major with a booming voice. Although he maintained a reputation as a strong disciplinarian among the troops he commanded, inside battalion headquarters he was funny and very human. After learning that my background included something about plants, he asked my advice on how we could get some color into the grounds—quickly and inexpensively. I recommended marigolds and assumed the planting would be limited to a raised bed outside the headquarters, but the major didn't do anything halfway. Soon he had commandeered compost and had troops working it into the soil and seeding marigolds around most of the Thirtieth Engineering Battalion buildings. By mid- to late summer, we had dazzling yellow and orange color everywhere!

Like most draftees, I kept a short-timer's calendar, checking off the days remaining in my two-year term. But, in retrospect, those two years of my life had positive elements. I became good friends with several of the other men and took advantage of the opportunity to visit the wealth of historical sites in the region with them. Mount Vernon was nearby, but we also drove the George Washington Memorial Parkway to visit Washington monuments and memorials, enjoyed the National Gallery of Art, and explored the gardens of Dumbarton Oaks in Georgetown. On some weekends we visited Civil War battlefield parks, including Manassas, Richmond, Fredericksburg, and even Gettysburg.

On January 20, 1961, we went to Washington on a snowy Inauguration Day and found a spot along Pennsylvania Avenue where we could watch the parade. John F. Kennedy and his brothers were tan and handsome and Jackie delicate and beautiful as they drove by in the open convertible.

3

EARLY FORAYS IN DESIGN

On my discharge from the army, I felt like the preliminaries were over and my professional life could begin. During my Fort Belvoir days, I had met Dawna Hauptman at Luther Place Memorial Church in Washington. She was in her final year at the School of Nursing at Washington Hospital Center, and we were heading toward marriage when she completed school. Soon after beginning my search for work, I learned of an open position in the Maryland–National Capital Park and Planning Commission in Silver Spring. After interviewing with Joseph Kondis, chief of the engineering and design division, I found myself with my first professional job as a designer.[1]

Within a few days, I had rented a furnished room on Philadelphia Avenue in nearby Takoma Park and begun commuting to Silver Spring and adjusting to the new office. My first assignment was to create site and grading plans for a series of tennis courts in Montgomery County parks. From that beginning, I moved on to do a planting plan for the new Wheaton Regional Park Riding Stables. My immaturity as a designer was perhaps best represented by the groups of three, five, and seven white and red pines I sprinkled around the site, believing that trees and shrubs should be planted in odd numbers. Then there were the forsythia I planted outside the riding ring.

The next planting plan assignment—for the site of the Maryland–National Capital Park and Planning Commission's new Wheaton Youth Center—gave me my first opportunity to design with predominantly native plants. Several mature white and northern red oak trees on the site had been preserved. I went back to my college textbook, Wyman's *Shrubs for American Gardens*, to find species adapted to the shade beneath the oaks. I chose spicebush, a native woodland shrub, and some native azaleas. But the concept of using native plant communities as a basis for design had not yet entered my world.

Over time, and with more experience, my life as a designer gradually began to change. I was now part of a group of fellow practitioners, and our daily lunches together significantly added to my professional development. Joe Kondis, my immediate supervisor, and his colleague Frank Kemple were both graduates of Pennsylvania State University's landscape architecture program and were eager to share their extensive knowledge. Joe had been a student of John R. Bracken, an early proponent of an ecological approach to landscape design, who introduced him to *American Plants for American Gardens* (1929).[2] This groundbreaking but little-known book was coauthored by the plant ecologist Edith Roberts and landscape architect Elsa Rehmann, who taught at Vassar in the 1920s.[3] Joe loaned me his copy, and once I opened the book, I couldn't put it down. The central message—that native plant communities provide the logical starting point for designing beautiful, functioning regional landscapes—would become central to my own design philosophy.

Each chapter of *American Plants for American Gardens* features a specific northeastern plant community. Informed by their extensive field observation, the authors discuss the key plant species in each group and the prevailing environmental conditions supporting them. These scientific observations, primarily the work of Roberts, are accompanied by Rehmann's vivid, poetic descriptions. The chapter "The Gray Birches" opens with the following:

> Wherever there are gray birches, Nature is in one of her lightest moods. These gray-white trees of slender form gather together in fairy-like groves. Their slim grace is accentuated by the way they often spring up in fives and sixes from a single root. When young they are gray-brown but later they are phantom white with black twigs and black notches. The effect is full of that mystery that etchings and delicate pencil drawings have. The gossamer quality is ever present; in the spring when their filmy foliage is light-filled, in summer when

their green is soft, in autumn when it is all sun-lit yellow, and even in the winter when the trees take on again their keynote colors from the snow and dark earth.[4]

The text is supplemented with comprehensive species lists of the trees, shrubs, vines, and ground layers typical of each of the twelve plant communities featured in the book. It seemed so logical to me, once Roberts and Rehmann pointed it out, that the native plant associations in a particular environment provide a basis for ecologically sound and aesthetically pleasing designed landscapes. This revelation motivated me to learn more about native plant communities and ecological processes in the living landscape.

In addition to opening my eyes to the wisdom and logic of Roberts and Rehmann's *American Plants for American Gardens,* Joe gave me work assign-

Gray birches on the trail to Schooner Cove, Acadia National Park, ME. Photograph by Nancy Houlihan.

"Wide-branched trees suggest a natural entrance," from *American Plants for American Gardens*.

ments that proved to be important in my ongoing education. One such opportunity was the field layout for a major planting project along the Montgomery County portion of Rock Creek Parkway. The planting was part of a belated implementation of a plan developed by the Olmsted firm.[5] My partner on this project was Frank Kemple, also a former student of John Bracken. Four years my senior, Frank was a great teacher for me, the neophyte on the team. The Olmsted plans showed the parkway alignment, the outline of existing canopy, and the approximate area on the plan for each planting, for example, "12 *Pinus strobus*," "8 *Cornus florida*," "42 *Corylus americana*." This information allowed us to stake precise locations of species' groupings in relation to site conditions. Within days of our pounding in the stakes, hundreds of trees and shrubs were planted in the locations that we had marked. Frank taught me his approach to "drifting" plants directionally within their groups, with one or more plants as "leaders" or "trailers" wandering beyond the others. This was a particularly satisfying project, both because we were working in the footsteps of the Olmsted firm and because of the immediate gratification of seeing the plan implemented. The trees we were placing ranged in size, and we could instantly see the value of varied heights within a grouping of a species. This was one of many projects in which I used the knowledge Joe and Frank passed on to me, as well as the wisdom in the pages of *American Plants for American Gardens*.

On November 22, 1963, I had just returned from lunch and was at my drafting table when Joe came into my office and said, "The president has been shot." That was all we heard initially. Radios were turned on, and about one thirty, the announcement came that President John F. Kennedy had died from an assassin's bullet in Dallas. Stunned, we silently put our drawing equipment away and quietly left the office. On Monday, November 25, I was downtown, along with thousands of others, watching the funeral procession. The sight of that riderless horse and Jackie walking in the procession will be forever etched in my memory.

After working with the Maryland–National Capital Park and Planning Commission from 1962 to 1964, I wanted to gain some experience in the private sector and found an opportunity in the Silver Spring office of Thurman Donovan & Associates.[6] My projects there were mostly planting plans for residential developments in Washington and the surrounding Maryland and Virginia suburbs, ranging from landscapes for medium-rise apartment buildings to single-family houses. In some cases, fragments of former forest communities remained on the building sites, but the species composition in the planting areas fit the "lawn-with-ornamental-trees-and-shrubs" tradition. For those projects, my planting plans incorporated some native understory trees, notably redbuds and flowering dogwoods. Characteristic shrubs were not so native: broad-leafed evergreens such as cherry laurel, Japanese and Chinese hollies, glossy privet, and Japanese azaleas. Where there was shade, a ground layer might be English ivy, periwinkle, or pachysandra in single-species blankets. It was during this period that my colleague Eric Sundback shared his insightful approach to garden design. Eric taught me how to make "moving spaces" by creating a mass:space plan as the first step in the design process, with the trees and shrub groups (the masses) forming baffles that partially conceal the spaces, which flow, river-like, between them.[7]

Two years later, in 1966, I moved on to a job with the District of Columbia Department of Highways and Traffic. When I arrived, the office was in the midst of highway "beautification" projects at the urging of Lady Bird Johnson. The First Lady had long been an effective proponent of such work in the Johnsons' home state of Texas, and it became a signature issue for her on a national scale when she and her family moved to the White House. The city of Washington benefited from her efforts, with street tree plantings, spring bulb displays, a major planting project along the South Capitol Street entrance into the city, and revitalized plantings around city libraries. Under the landscape architect Ralph D'Amato's leadership, I participated in the design of several of these projects beginning in fall 1966.

During this interlude, I benefited from an easy commute—a twenty-minute train ride to Union Station and a short walk to the Ford Building on Pennsylvania Avenue—as well as access to cultural treasures. I often ate my brown bag lunch in a small triangular park across from my office and adjacent to the National Gallery. The remainder of my lunch hour was spent exploring the gallery's rooms of French impressionist and cubist paintings. During such quiet moments, standing before Monets, Van Goghs, and Picassos, I aspired to something more in my own work. I wanted to gain a stronger base in the type of ecological design so eloquently expressed in *American Plants for American Gardens* and, to that end, began to explore the possibility of enrolling in graduate school.

By then, I was married to Dawna, now a registered nurse, and had a son, one-year-old Jon. The search for a graduate program led to a family road trip to the University of Wisconsin–Madison in the fall of 1966. There I met Bill Tishler, then an assistant professor in the planning and landscape architecture department, who told me about a graduate research assistantship funded by a federal grant he had been awarded. The project involved developing design and planning guidelines for Bayfield, a charming hillside town on the shores of Lake Superior in northern Wisconsin. Bayfield was the jumping-off point for the newly designated Apostle Islands National Lakeshore, and the project goal was to work with civic leaders to protect the town's unique character in the face of an influx of tourists and new development. When Tishler announced that the two-year assistantship was mine if I wanted it, the possibility of graduate school became a reality. In addition to my educational benefits through the Veterans Administration, I was supported by Dawna, who would work part-time as a registered nurse while pursuing a bachelor's degree in nursing.

4

MERGING ECOLOGY
WITH DESIGN

During graduate school, I became aware of the pioneering work in ecological restoration that had begun in the early 1930s at the newly established University of Wisconsin Arboretum. From its beginning, the founders envisioned their project as unique in its effort to restore entire plant communities. At the arboretum's dedication on June 17, 1934, the environmentalist and author Aldo Leopold described this goal as "in a nutshell . . . to reconstruct . . . a sample of original Wisconsin—a sample of what Dane County looked like when our ancestors arrived here in the 1840s."[1] Within a year of the dedication, Civilian Conservation Corps workers were planting the arboretum's Curtis Prairie—the first restored prairie in the world.

In 1967, thirty-two years after the launching of this groundbreaking restoration project, I was a new graduate student in the university's summer session. The first course I took was Botany 450, Plant Ecology. In field labs at Curtis Prairie, we laid out sampling plots, noting species presence, frequency, and density. I saw some of my old friends from the Iowa roadside—pale purple coneflowers, beebalm, and delicate pink prairie roses—but also discovered species that were new to me and learned to appreciate the subtle beauty of fine-textured grasses and sedges. Soon I began to see patterns in different species' distribution: the tendency of some to be highly aggregated and others to be sprinkled more randomly. In his *Sand County Almanac*, Leopold

Mesic prairie section with Curtis Prairie beyond, Native Plant Garden, University of Wisconsin–Madison Arboretum. Photograph by Robert Jaeger.

Historic Greene Prairie restoration, UW Arboretum. Photograph by Darrel Morrison.

Central vista, Native Plant Garden, UW Arboretum, showing wetland, mesic prairies, bur oak savanna (*right*), black oak savanna (*left*), and oak-hickory forest. Photograph by Robert Jaeger.

eloquently expresses this process of education, noting that "our ability to perceive quality in nature begins, as in art, with the pretty. It expands through successive stages of the beautiful to values as yet uncaptured by language."[2] For me, the next step involved thinking about the processes that led to patterns: microenvironmental differences, varying means of reproduction, plant migration, competition, and succession.

The text for the plant ecology class was John T. Curtis's *The Vegetation of Wisconsin*, published in 1959, shortly before his premature death. The book is a lasting legacy, reflecting the author's encyclopedic knowledge of Wiscon-

White wild indigo and spiderwort in mesic prairie section, Native Plant Garden, UW Arboretum. Photograph by Robert Jaeger.

sin's native plant communities and detailed studies in the plant ecology lab he established in 1946. *The Vegetation of Wisconsin* covers twenty-one major plant communities, with quantitative data gained from sampling a number of stands in each type. For me, and many others, it was the bible. After reading about the communities, I spent time immersed in the arboretum prairies, experiencing their color, texture, and movement. Over time, I became increasingly inspired by the idea of bringing those qualities into designed landscapes.[3]

Throughout the next two years of graduate school, I discovered other sources of inspiration. In fall 1967, I came upon *The Tropical Gardens of Burle Marx* in a local bookstore.[4] I put it on my Christmas list, and my parents gave me a copy that year. The Brazilian artist and landscape architect Roberto Burle Marx's dramatic landscapes, artistic compositions he "painted with plants," swept me away. An artist and a botanist, he merged both callings in his work. With the French ecologist Henrique Lahmeyer de Mello Barreto, Burle Marx led other designers and botanists on *coletas,* or plant-collecting trips, in the interior of Brazil. He propagated newly discovered species and incorporated many of them in his designed landscapes. I marveled over the rich compositions he created with plants which appeared in the pages of *Landscape Architecture Magazine* throughout the 1960s.

It was also in the pages of *Landscape Architecture* that I first came upon the work of A. E. Bye. In 1967, I read his unforgettable essay "Landscape Luminosity," in which he described placing plants with translucent foliage where they would be backlit during part of the day and become "luminous." It came as no surprise to me that Bye had been a student of John Bracken at Penn State. The magazine also included articles on Bye's current design projects in Connecticut, accompanied by his black-and-white photographs of subtly rich landscapes.[5]

A year after I arrived at the university, an unexpected faculty resignation during the summer of 1968 led to the immediate need for an instructor to teach the fall undergraduate planting design class. Although I hardly felt qualified as a lecturer, I was available and selected to fill the position. The details of how I would split my time between my research assistantship duties and my teaching assignment (while also writing a master's thesis) were tentatively worked out, though balancing these responsibilities would prove a delicate, and at times exhausting, experience. To compensate for my lack of confidence lecturing, I spent long hours preparing for each class. It must have been trying for my students to sit through those tedious, heavily prepped lectures, but I certainly increased my knowledge while trying to teach them.

The prescribed curriculum in the Wisconsin landscape architecture program included courses on woody plants and their identification, taught in the horticulture department. Students learned the palette of trees, shrubs, and vines that I knew from Donald Wyman's books, but there were no courses on herbaceous plants, and certainly none on native herbaceous plants as components of native plant communities. I saw this gap in the curriculum as an opportunity to devote a portion of my planting design class to studying the forests and restored prairies that had inspired me as a new grad student. We took field trips to the arboretum's prairie, savanna, and forest communities, identifying key species along the way, sometimes sketching them, and often noting characteristic distribution patterns or phenomena such as Bye's landscape luminosity. In the studio component of the course, I assigned projects such as "Design of a Small Woodland Garden" or "Design of a Dry Prairie Garden," in which students used plant species they had met along the trails in the arboretum.

The next step for me was to propose and develop a new course in landscape architecture, Native Plant Communities of Wisconsin, a combination of lectures and field labs in which we looked at environmental characteristics, botanical composition, and aesthetic qualities of a broad cross section of Wisconsin plant communities. Fortuitously, in 1973 the university initiated a new three-week intersession between spring semester and the eight-week summer session. It was intended as a total-immersion experience, where students could earn three academic credits in three weeks—a format custom-made for an intensive field class. The seed for such an experiment had been planted when

Ox-eye (*left*); butterfly weed, little bluestem, and flowering spurge. Photographs by Susan Carpenter.

Northern Wisconsin spruce-fir forest and bog complex. Photograph by Darrel Morrison.

I was in the wilds of Fort Hood, Texas, fantasizing about studying the surrounding native landscape. Approval of this course, which merged fieldwork and classroom instruction, marked the beginning of a new stage in my teaching career.

I taught the course solo for a couple of years, with classes from 8 a.m. to 5 p.m., five days a week. The first two weeks, we made day trips in university vans to southern Wisconsin prairies, savannas, forests, and wetlands. Many of the sites we visited were State Scientific Areas, for which plant species lists were available. The third week we were in residence in northern Wisconsin, usually staying at Kemp Natural Resources Station. From there, we traveled to northern forests, bogs, and sedge meadows.

In 1975, the plant ecologist Evelyn Howell joined the faculty, and the two of us co-taught the course for the next nine years. We became, in a way, a Wisconsin version of the team of Edith Roberts and Elsa Rehmann. Between us, we merged science with art. We performed quantitative studies, laying out quadrats (sampling plots) and line transects, identifying species in them, then calculat-

Cinnamon fern, near Marinette, northern Wisconsin. Photograph by Darrel Morrison.

Wetland in Avoca Prairie, Iowa County, WI. Photograph by Darrel Morrison.

ing frequencies, cover, and density. In sampling ground layer, teams of three or four students examined meter-square quadrats on hands and knees. In sampling forest communities, we laid out hundred-square-meter circular quadrats, and collected data from them to determine the relative importance and abundance of tree and shrub species and to observe their distribution patterns and spacing. These scientific methods were balanced with artistic ones: drawing quick sketches of individual plants, leaves, and flowers or graphically capturing the "visual essence" of the community type by portraying characteristic aesthetic elements such as line, form, color, and texture. We invoked quiet time, sometimes immediately upon entering a particular community stand, asking each student to find a spot to be alone and to write about what they were seeing, hearing, smelling, and feeling. We gave students the option of reading what they had written when we reassembled. These readings were often pure poetry.

The three-week sessions within the naturally evolving landscape were invaluable, both for the class and for us. When I made pronouncements about such things as the desirability of having gently curving paths versus straight paths in the woods or prairie, Evelyn pinned me down by asking tough questions like "*Why* is the curving path better?" I remember my answer to that one: "Because the view is always changing on a curving path."

While we were immersed in learning, we also enjoyed ourselves. Being in the field brought out some of my bad plant puns, such as one I repeated whenever we came upon a luxuriant fern: "with fronds like that, who needs anemones?" Evelyn and I made up contests like "timed walks," where teams of two students listed all the species they could find within a ten-minute period. During the third week of the course, the "Up North" week at Kemp Station, we assigned cooking teams to prepare breakfasts and dinners. The culinary competition was keen, with each team trying to outdo the previous day's achievements. We ate very well, dining and enjoying wine by candlelight. In the evenings, we collated data from the day's sampling exercises and discussed "the question of the day." On occasion there were after-dinner games of "plant charades," in which students acted out plant names (Latin or common). These could be hilarious and even a bit risqué. How do you portray Virginia creeper, naked sunflower, or wild leek?

By this time I had come to "know" the Danish-born landscape architect Jens Jensen—the person who most influenced me as a teacher and designer. I never met Jensen, although our lives overlapped by fourteen years.[6] I was still a boy on the farm in Iowa when he died at the age of ninety-one at his school, The Clearing, in Ellison Bay, Door County, Wisconsin. Two of my faculty colleagues who had firsthand knowledge of Jensen introduced me to him and his work. Bill Tishler, my major professor, had grown up in Door County in the 1940s and remembered seeing Jensen as a distinguished elderly gentleman in his home town, Bailey's Harbor. George Ziegler, a landscape architect for the university extension service, visited The Clearing multiple times while an undergraduate in the University of Wisconsin program. George and I frequently had lunch together, and his recollections of Jensen and The Clearing often came up in conversations. He recalled working in the school's gardens and fields with fellow students, eating meals with Jensen in the dining room, and gathering around the lodge fireplace in the evening to listen to Jensen expound on landscapes and life.

The Lodge, The Clearing, Ellison Bay, WI. Photograph by Bonnie Harper-Lore.

It was George who introduced me to Jensen's book *Siftings*, published in 1939, and to Leonard Eaton's more recent book about him, *Landscape Artist in America,* published in 1964. From the biography, I learned that Jensen was born in the Slesvig province in Denmark before it was forcibly annexed to Germany. In 1884, he emigrated to the United States with his wife-to-be, Anne Marie Hansen. From his early days in Chicago, Jensen developed a friendship with the plant ecologist Henry Cowles. He and the University of Chicago professor spent many hours together exploring regional prairies and forests as well as the Indiana Dunes in Gary, Indiana.[7] Cowles's fame as a pioneer in the new science of ecology increased over the decades, and he became a mentor to many, including Edith Roberts, who earned her PhD at the university in 1915.

Over three decades, Jensen worked in the Chicago parks, rising from laborer to superintendent of the West Park System, and in addition to his notable park design work, had a long and prolific career practicing from his Ravinia studio. His clientele, a Who's Who of early twentieth-century industrialists, included Henry Ford, for whom he designed Fair Lane, in Dearborn, Michigan. After Jensen's wife died in 1934, he closed his office and moved to Ellison Bay. Here, with the assistance of his secretary, Mertha Fulkerson, Jensen established his "School of the Soil," The Clearing. From The Clearing, he continued his design practice with such masterful works as Lincoln Memorial Garden in Springfield, Illinois, in the mid-1930s, and Glenwood Children's Park in Madison, a decade later. *Siftings*, published four years after he moved to The Clearing, is filled with wisdom that has remained with me since I first read the book almost five decades ago.

On curves in the landscape:

Parks and gardens of curves are always new, always revealing new thoughts and new interests in life. . . . Landscaping must follow the lines of the free-growing tree with its thousands of curves.[8]

On white birch trees:

Birches and moonlight are real companions. No other tree speaks so beautifully as the birch in full moonlight.[9]

On council rings, which Jensen included in many of his designs:

In this friendly circle, around the fire, man becomes himself. Here there is no social caste. All are on the same level, looking each other in the face. A ring speaks of strength and friendship and is one of the great symbols of mankind.[10]

After reading the chapter of Eaton's book devoted to The Clearing, I knew it was time for my first pilgrimage to the 128-acre site above limestone cliffs rising up from the Green Bay side of Lake Michigan. The site was a mosaic of maple-beech forests, young birch and aspen stands, pastures, and abandoned fields, with a spectacular view over the water. In addition to locating the school buildings, pathways, and drives, Jensen designated features such as "sun openings," vistas of Green Bay to the west, and a "pathway to the rising sun" on the winter solstice. Along with the unique natural beauty of the place, I would see Jensen's hand in its landscape design.

In May 1970, as my first year of full-time teaching neared an end, I arranged a visit to The Clearing with my undergraduate class in planting design. Clair and Dorothy Johnson, resident managers, planned a dinner for us and assembled a remarkable group of guests: Mertha Fulkerson, Jensen's secretary who served as the school's director from his death in 1951 until she retired in 1969; her sister, Ada Corson, a frequent visitor at The Clearing; Elizabeth Gimmler, a landscape architect who had worked for Jensen in the Ravinia office; "Miss Emma" Toft, an ardent Door County conservationist and close friend of Jensen; and Sid and Inez Telfer, orchardists who lived nearby and were friends of the school. Throughout this memorable evening, the guests told stories of Jensen and his work, adding personal details such as his proclivity for a shot of akvavit before going to bed each night. Mertha especially enjoyed telling the story of the falling out between Jensen and Frank Lloyd Wright. The two had collaborated on projects in the past, and despite their differences, Jensen generally respected Wright for his architectural skill. However, after the end of World War II, Wright wrote Jensen asking for a letter recommending him as the architect to review and approve the designs for all US State Department buildings. Jensen didn't think anyone should have that much power and ignored the request. Wright wrote a second letter asking for

Three pines, Lodge Meadow, The Clearing, Ellison Bay, WI. Photograph courtesy The Clearing.

Jensen's endorsement, and again he ignored it. Finally, after receiving Wright's third request, he asked Mertha to type an unusually succinct response: "Go to Hell."

The weekend field trip whetted my appetite for more time at The Clearing. The next summer, I signed up for a one-week course on the native vegetation of Door County taught by Floyd Swink, a taxonomist at the Morton Arboretum in Lisle, Illinois. Swink not only had an encyclopedic knowledge of regional plants but also shared my love of puns. He was known to expound on intricacies like the fact that there is not only a white baneberry with

Inner Meadow, The Clearing, Ellison Bay, WI. Photograph courtesy The Clearing.

white fruits, and a red baneberry with red fruits, but also a red-fruited white baneberry and a white-fruited red baneberry. Seeing two insects on a leaf, he would point to the smaller of the two and say, "the lesser of two weevils."[11]

During the week, I stayed in the men's dorm—a log structure that Jensen had moved to The Clearing years earlier to become a part of the central building complex. We spent mornings on the property, learning characteristic plants in rocky oldfields with their oldfield junipers and sumacs; early-successional forests with closely spaced aspens and birches; forests with multi-aged sugar maples dominating; and mature forests of maples, aging yellow birches, hemlocks, and beeches. There were shrubs at the edges of the forests: round-leaf dogwoods, filberts, and buffalo berries. The ground beneath some of the forest canopies was carpeted with woodland ferns and wildflowers: Canada mayflower, wild sarsaparilla, bigleaf aster, blue cohosh, Solomon's seal, false Solomon's seal, partridge berry, and, yes, both red and white baneberries in all their variations.

At the western edge of The Clearing property, white limestone cliffs plunged a hundred feet down to the waters of Green Bay. Ancient arborvitae, or white cedars, in gnarled, sculptural forms, clung to ledges on the cliffs and lined the rocky trail we followed along the top. In the first chapter of *Siftings*, Jensen refers to that trail:

Trails are the footprints of the ages. They mark the history of man. One of these trails, like a silvery thread winding its way over precipitous cliffs, still leads to my pioneer log house. The Indian, on hunting expeditions or in conflict with other tribes, trod this trail, because from here he could see afar. Pioneers followed him for adventure and for gain. But it was love of the primitive that led us

Trail along the Escarpment, The Clearing, Ellison Bay, WI. Photograph courtesy The Clearing.

Morrison at Toft Point, Bailey's Harbor, WI, 1980. Photograph by Bonnie Harper-Lore.

here. It is a storm-beaten trail, where the elements roar and shriek in their fury.[12]

In Floyd Swink's class, we trod this trail and many others, including those covered with a deep layer of sawdust, making them the most comfortable trails I have ever walked. Mornings flew by as we studied The Clearing's plants. At 11:50 a.m. each day, a bell rang outside the kitchen, calling us in for dinner at noon. After the big midday meal, the class loaded into students' cars to visit natural areas with plants not represented at The Clearing. These were places such as The Ridges Sanctuary at Bailey's Harbor, which Jensen, Miss Emma Toft, and others had fought to save as a nature preserve in perpetuity, and nearby Toft Point, a virgin, pine-dominated forest that Miss Emma and her family had protected for decades, now a State Natural Area. Absorbed in learning more plants in such unique natural preserves, we often had to hurry back to reach The Clearing in time for supper.

The week at The Clearing inspired me to develop my own course on Jensen and his work, which I taught the following summer and, with variations, alternate summers until 2003. In the afternoons, we went on field trips to many of the sites I had come to know in Swink's company. After identifying plants, we tried to capture the aesthetic essence of the different landscapes through drawings. On one trip to Toft Point, as the class looked out over a meadow with butterflies flitting among drifts of coreopsis, one student observed that "you landscape people should put butterflies in all of your landscapes." Four decades later, professional landscape designers are consciously designing "pollinator" gardens that benefit both the pollinators and the people who enjoy these landscapes filled with life and movement.

My students took part in the long-standing tradition of doing physical labor

Watercolor by Morrison, Toft Point, Bailey's Harbor, WI, 1997.

at The Clearing on Fridays. Our work projects usually took the form of "editing"—removing volunteer vegetation that obscured Jensen's planned vistas and views or encroached on sun openings through the trees. In addition to perpetuating Jensen's spatial design, this editing taught us the potential value of "design by subtraction," with immediate results. One of our goals was to leave a site so that the casual observer passing through would never notice our intervention.

Friday nights at The Clearing were traditionally a time for student presentations, to which neighbors and friends of the school were invited. The students pinned up landscape designs they had done during the week and prepared original skits, like "The Twelve Days of Landscape" that ended with "a partridgeberry under yon tree." On another occasion, they presented *Beauty of the Wild*, a masque by the playwright Kenneth Sawyer Goodman. The short play laments the disappearance of Nature, which is symbolized by a faun. Land occupied by wildlife and Native people is being invaded and destroyed by hunters and industrialists. The faun feels hopeless, but in the end a sympathetic friend reassures the faun that people can in fact provide protection. The play was performed as a "conservation play" at sites that Jensen and others believed should be protected, sometimes attracting audiences of hundreds. The audience for my class's production was somewhat smaller.

Another tradition at The Clearing was for classes to gather around the council ring above the cliffs for libations before supper, or afterward for a campfire, stories and songs, sunset-watching, and perhaps, more libations. It was never completely clear to me whether the beverages were officially sanctioned, but Jens would have approved. That he enjoyed life is attested to in photographs of him in a playful mood, standing on his head, and doing a circle dance with friends at Indiana Dunes. In honor of him, some of my classes were inspired to join hands and do a similar dance when we found ourselves on a sandy beach like the one at Bailey's Harbor, after an afternoon of botanizing and sketching in The Ridges. Jens would have joined in.

During the thirty years that I taught at The Clearing, between 1973 and 2003, a grand piano and a pump organ stood in the living room of the main lodge, where students assembled before breakfast, dinner, and supper. Although I didn't have the audacity to play while students gathered for meals, I did sneak in occasionally late in the evening to play my favorite composition by the Norwegian composer Edvard Grieg, "Wedding Day at Troldhaugen."

Council Ring, The Clearing, Ellison Bay, WI. Photograph courtesy The Clearing.

The piano and organ were reminders of how much Jensen valued music. In *Siftings*, he wrote:

> To me the art of landscaping is more closely associated with music than any other art. Its rhythm and its tonal qualities are as a folk song or a sonata. In its greatness it might be a symphony. For a friend, I planted a group of sumac on a hillock facing the setting sun. When autumn's frosty breath turned their leafy crowns into a flaming red, my friend called it the "*Tännhauser* Group."[13]

Near the north property line of The Clearing, Jensen built his rustic "cliff house" into the limestone cliffs that drop precipitously to the waters of Green

Bay. To get to the tiny building, one follows the "storm-beaten trail" Jensen described in *Siftings*. One June, I happened to be teaching at The Clearing on my birthday and was given the key to the Cliff House, where I would stay overnight as a special treat. After supper, I followed the rocky trail through the gnarled arborvitaes on top of the cliff, and clambered down stone steps to the door, unlocked it, and laid out my sleeping bag on the rickety cot. There was a rustic birch table in front of a pair of casement windows that opened out to the view of Green Bay. As it was getting dark, I lit a couple of candles on the fireplace mantel and savored the moments in Jensen's retreat. Thunderheads appeared in the sky over the bay, but all was calm when I blew out the candles and crawled into my sleeping bag. The rhythmic waves washed the stone-covered beach below. During the night, I awoke to a full-blown storm, with wind, thunder, lightning, and crashing waves battering the cliffs below. I received the full treatment of the elements' "roaring and shrieking in their fury." It was one of my most memorable birthday celebrations.

In 1973, I made an exciting discovery at The Clearing unrelated to the site's physical landscape or natural characteristics. Bill Kasakaitas of the Wisconsin Farm Bureau Federation, The Clearing's steward at the time, asked that I go through the school building and look for drawings and papers that should be stored in a secure, climate-controlled environment. I started my search in the large studio/classroom, where flat wooden files contained many of Jensen's original drawings, and then went through a corner cabinet in Mertha Fulkerson's weaving room, where I found several Friends of Our Native Landscape publications and copies of some of Jensen's letters that had been typed by Mertha.[14] (I didn't find the "Go to Hell" letter.) As I climbed the ladder up to the balcony overlooking the large studio, I discovered a dark wooden cabinet wedged deep under the sharply sloping ceiling. To my amazement, the drawers were filled with black-and-white photographs (and negatives) of Jensen project sites from 1900 to the 1930s, as well as pictures of groups on field trips, most likely members of the Friends of Our Native Landscape. My heart pounded as I realized this was the photographic collection that Jensen himself thought had burned in the 1937 lodge fire.

The next day, Bill and I loaded up the trove of drawings and correspondence, along with the long-lost photographs, and brought the collection back to Madison. Subsequently, Steve Christy, a landscape architecture graduate student, catalogued the new materials and used them in research for his master's thesis, "The Growth of an Artist: Jens Jensen and Landscape Architecture." The collection was deposited in the Morton Arboretum library, which already held a major Jensen collection, curated by Carol Doty. During the summer of 1981, another fire at The Clearing gutted much of the school building's interior, including the balcony that had sheltered the wooden cabinet.

Looking back at those early years as an assistant professor at Wisconsin, I see how my experiences converged in a way that informed both my teaching and my practice. The pioneering restoration efforts at the arboretum; field instruction in natural areas; study of Roberto Burle Marx, A. E. Bye, and especially Jens Jensen; and the opportunity to experience The Clearing not only inspired my teaching but also opened up new design opportunities for me and my students. One of these was brought to my attention by student residents of the Zoe Bayliss Women's Cooperative dormitory, who protested a plan to convert the vacant lot next to their building into a parking lot as an interim use before construction of a traffic interchange. This was also a community project since the plot was owned jointly by the university and the city of Madison. In 1971, the co-op won approval from the campus planning committee to develop a park there, with the understanding that it might be replaced once plans for the interchange moved forward. When the residents of Zoe Bayliss came to the landscape architecture department and me for assistance in developing the park, I assigned the project to a small group of graduate students in my planting design class. They met with representatives of the co-op, and the concept of a predominantly native landscape emerged from the discussion, becoming the theme for a design competition among the students. Jodi Geiger's winning project featured a broad path winding by a sunny prairie slope, with early-successional trembling aspen, staghorn sumac, and red cedars in the upper part of the park and a mix of oaks, maples, and woodland shrubs in the lower part. Along the pathway, "bays" of mown grass provided areas for seating.

The project, named Walden Park, benefited from the growing interest in the environment, spearheaded by Wisconsin senator Gaylord Nelson, following the first Earth Day, April 22, 1970. The UW Arboretum and private

Walden Park prairie planting area, Madison, WI, 1974. Photograph by Darrel Morrison.

sources donated the trees and shrubs. Prairie plants were propagated from locally collected seed in horticulture department greenhouses; all of the planting was done by volunteers in spring 1972. Since the park was installed, Park Street has been widened, reducing the area by about 25 percent, and the sign incorporating Thoreau's famous quotation "In wildness is the preservation of the world" was a casualty of that decision. Nevertheless, for almost fifty years, Walden Park has brought a touch of wildness into a very urban area.

After reading about Walden Park in the local newspaper, Sam Harper, vice president of CUNA (Credit Union National Association) Mutual Insurance Company, contacted me about consulting on a landscape plan that would refer to the native southern Wisconsin landscape. CUNA Mutual was in the midst of a major building expansion at its headquarters in Madison, and the twelve-acre site would need to be redeveloped. My design drew on Jens Jensen's lessons of mass and space, on the sweeping forms of Roberto Burle Marx, and on prairie restoration techniques gained from the pioneering work at the arboretum. The plan also incorporated native forest and forest-edge species to enclose and surround large open areas, which themselves featured sweeps of native prairie grasses and forbs surrounding mowed turf. Trees and shrubs were planted by a contractor in fall 1972. We also planted oats as a cover crop that year, and the next June, I hand-broadcast prairie species there with Cathie Bruner, a UW horticulture student. Our planting plan included some sweeping swaths of prairie grasses on the rooftop of a parking garage. A few years later, in 1975, Grady Clay, the longtime editor of *Landscape Architecture Magazine,* invited me to write an article for a special issue with the theme "The Search for a Native Landscape." I featured Walden Park and CUNA Mutual as case studies in my article "Restoring the Midwestern Landscape."[15]

Newspaper coverage of the Walden Park and CUNA Mutual projects in 1972 and 1973 led to an invitation to design a plan for a prairie landscape at the eighty-acre corporate site of General Electric's Medical Systems Division at Pewaukee, just west of Milwaukee. This exciting opportunity was also daunting. The two acres of prairie planting at CUNA Mutual seemed insignificant in comparison to a property half the size of "our place"—the 160-acre Iowa farm. In addition to scale, I would be planting on GE's disturbed site, which was bordered on the south by Interstate 94. The massive building under con-

Prairie area with switchgrass and big bluestem, GE Medical Systems Division, Pewaukee, WI. Photograph by Darrel Morrison.

struction required grading to accommodate large, impervious parking areas that drained into swales. Non-native vegetation had invaded former cropland. As a starting point for the restoration project, I spent days walking over the eighty acres, making notes on topographic maps and soil surveys.

After compiling my field notes, I developed seed mixes matched with the varying conditions and determined seed quantities for each zone. There were commercial sources for commonly occurring native grasses but not for more specialized species, such as northern prairie cordgrass—the "slough grass" on the Iowa farm—with its miraculous ability to withstand flooding and fluctuating moisture levels. Because seed of most of the forbs I wanted to incorporate was not generally available in large quantities, I spent many September and October weekends in 1974 on seed-collecting trips with nine-year-old Jon. This was our version of the deer- or duck-hunting commonly done by father-and-son teams. General Electric also paid my students to collect seed of species I designated, mainly from roadsides and railroad rights-of-way. The pressure of gathering sufficient forb seed mounted, and as our deadline loomed, I tossed and turned in bed at night, envisioning seed blown

First controlled burn of prairie, GE Medical Systems Division, Pewaukee, WI, 1980. Photograph by Darrel Morrison.

Prairie area with early-successional forbs, GE Medical Systems Division, Pewaukee, WI, 1980. Photograph by Darrel Morrison.

away or washed down the stalks of prairie species during storms. We ultimately succeeded in hand collecting sixty pounds during that fall.

The next spring, a contractor was hired to drill various grass seed mixes
in zones I had flagged. Then forb mixes of five to ten species were overseeded
in drifts. The GE planting grew slowly at first, but its growth pattern soon
followed the prairie planter's oft-repeated adage: "The first year it sleeps;
the second year it creeps; the third year it LEAPS." During those early years
at GE, the landscape increasingly resembled a prairie, but the turning point
came at the beginning of the fifth growing season, in spring 1980, when we
conducted the first major controlled burn. With our burn that spring, we were
simply emulating a natural process that human populations had long utilized

to stimulate native growth by putting nutrients into the soil in a usable form, by earlier warming of the blackened soil, by suppressing woody species that would potentially shade out the native grasses, and even reducing the flea and tick population during the summer after a burn. The skeptical corporate leadership had to be convinced of the value of fire and our ability to contain it. In response to GE's concerns, we pointed out that existing paved drives and mowed areas would act as built-in fire breaks and called for additional mowing around the periphery. On the first Saturday of May 1980, a group of students and corporate executives were assembled to conduct the burn. I invited some of the latter to ignite the fire by dragging burning brooms around the periphery. The experience led several of them to become advocates of prairie fires (and prairies more generally).

If the General Electric site was disturbed, the next site I found myself involved with was downright hostile to plant growth. For decades, iron ore tailings had been deposited in this 320-acre circular area, part of the Jackson County Iron Company's operation near Black River Falls, Wisconsin. In 1979, I initiated a research project to develop techniques to revegetate and stabilize the tailings deposits using USDA funding under the 1887 Hatch Act, administered by the College of Agricultural and Life Sciences. The layers of tailings had created a brutal environment, with summer surface temperatures up to 140 degrees F, low nutrient availability, almost no organic matter, a high pH, and a soil texture equivalent to sandy loam. Without intervention, the tailings basin would remain bare for decades, subject to water and wind erosion, which in turn would impact a much larger area. Our project experimented with using different levels of fertilizers and a uniform seed mix in meter-square quadrats laid out in the tailings basin. The fertilizer treatments were developed with guidance from UW soil scientists. The species selection was based on hunches—my observations of native prairie species that seemed especially well adapted to heat, drought, and disturbance. We were effectively setting into motion a process of natural succession in an unnatural environment.[16]

The real nitty-gritty work on this project was done by graduate assistants, as is often the case, beginning with Julie Hardell, who laid out and monitored the first set of plots and collected and analyzed data from them at the end of the season. The following year, Gretel Hengst applied the same rate and composition of fertilizer to the plots and continued measurement of growth and cover.

By the end of the 1980 growing season, vegetative cover in the plots ranged from 40 percent to more than 90 percent, and plant succession was moving ahead. No additional fertilizer was applied to the plots after the 1980 growing season.

The best-performing native grass in 1979 and 1980 was Canada wildrye, whose seed happened to come from the sandy banks of the Wisconsin River near Baraboo. I had had the good fortune of hand collecting the seed there at the invitation of Nina Leopold Bradley, daughter of Aldo Leopold. On a sunny Saturday morning in 1978, Nina and I were accompanied by her good friend Amy Roosevelt, niece of Franklin Delano and Eleanor Roosevelt and grand-niece of Teddy Roosevelt. Amy, an educator and avid environmentalist, was visiting from Colorado when the three of us collected wildrye seed a few hundred feet from the "shack" where Aldo Leopold is reported to have written *A Sand County Almanac*. It was an honor to be with these two stalwart conservationists, and fitting that the species whose seed we had collected performed so well as a "healing" plant in Jackson County, helping to bring back Leopold's "integrity, stability and beauty" to this drastically disturbed environment.

The experimental work went on. Peter Lindquist, a graduate student, planted another set of plots in the tailings basin in 1980. When Tom Hunt, a consultant to Jackson County Iron Company, joined the team in 1982, he designed and oversaw the installation of a field-scale planting, employing knowledge gained from the experimental plots.[17] After Jackson closed in 1989, the mine site was turned over to the Jackson County Department of Forestry and Parks for a county facility, Wazee Lake Park. Tom, by then professor and director of reclamation studies at the University of Wisconsin–Platteville, consulted as planner for the park from 1983 to 1992. The park is now an important recreation area and wildlife preserve that includes among its residents a wolf pack, an elk herd, and the federally endangered Karner blue butterfly, all living in a complex of forests and restored prairies.

Meanwhile, back on the Madison campus during summer 1981, the Department of Landscape Architecture hosted the annual meeting of CELA, the Council of Educators in Landscape Architecture, at its conference center overlooking Lake Mendota. At the meeting, I proposed that CELA establish a peer-reviewed scholarly journal. I had prepared the proposal in talks with Steve Miller, director of the journals division of the University of Wisconsin Press, who laid out a plan for making such an endeavor financially viable for CELA.

Steve's enthusiasm and support led to the press's initial subsidization and publication of the new semiannual *Landscape Journal*. In retrospect, my proposal was audacious, since I was without experience in the intricacies of scholarly publication. Fortunately, my colleague Arne Alanen joined me as founding co-editor, and graduate student Signe Holtz became our editorial assistant. In the four decades of its life thus far, *Landscape Journal*'s home and editorial staff have rotated on to other schools, but Arne continues as a consulting editor.

I worked long hours during the 1970s on many professional pursuits and owe much to Dawna for taking Jon and his little brother Scott, born in 1972, to soccer and hockey practice, attending PTA meetings, and keeping the home fires burning as I climbed the academic ladder and developed an obsession for running. Two of my neighbors had encouraged me to join the Vilas Running Club, a group of university professors who convened at the UW natatorium each weekday, year-round, to go on long-distance runs. It was slow-going at first, but over time, I began to improve and eventually ran in many road races, including one marathon. Running came relatively easily, and after a youth of failing at sports, it gave me a physical challenge that helped balance my academic life.

In late fall 1982, I received a letter inviting me to apply for the position of dean of the School of Environmental Design at the University of Georgia. The invitation surprised me, but I also found it enticing. There is a syndrome that sometimes afflicts those in academia, urging them to move up to administration in that community. I had gone through various stages up to that point: assistant professor to associate professor with tenure, to professor, and then to a three-year term as departmental chair. One logical next step would be to become an associate dean or dean of a school or college. I always felt that I had slid into my first teaching appointment at Wisconsin by chance, and now the possibility of competing for a deanship at an unfamiliar school was intriguing—a test to see if I could succeed on my own merits.

At the end of the year, I decided to throw my hat into the ring and submitted my application. A long waiting period followed. With time to reflect, I acknowledged that my first love was designing landscapes and passing on this passion to students, especially by teaching about the link between ecology and design. But just when I had abandoned the idea of a move to the Deep South, I was invited for an interview. After seeing a list of the other candidates, I became convinced that my interview was purely a formality, necessary to meet university requirements. But why not take a trip to Georgia? Late spring would be in full swing there, with flowering dogwoods, azaleas, and magnolias in bloom. It would be an opportunity to see my Georgia colleagues Ian J. W. Firth, Catherine Howett, Richard Westmacott, and Allen Stovall as well as to indulge in some fine southern food.

So, without the pressure of thinking I might actually be selected, I relaxed and enjoyed meeting university administrators, conversing with the Environmental Design faculty, even answering questions like "Are you tough enough to be a dean?" and felt uncharacteristically at ease as I gave my lecture, "Landscapes That Have Influenced Me/Landscapes That I Have Influenced." On the second night of the two-day interview, after having dinner with the graduate students, I walked the length of the campus. On the old North Campus, I admired the university's most historic buildings, Demosthenian Hall, the Chapel, Old College. Majestic glossy-leaved southern magnolias, native to southern Georgia, were in bloom with creamy-white flowers, nearly a foot across, exuding their never-to-be-forgotten aroma. I flew home to Madison the next morning, ran in a twenty-mile road race, and began preparing handouts for the three-week intersession field course on Wisconsin native plant communities that Evelyn and I would teach in a few weeks.

When a letter arrived offering me the deanship, I found myself facing a life-changing decision. Accepting the offer would upend my family's life and immerse us in a new, unknown world. I would need to study unfamiliar landscapes and take on a new set of responsibilities. At the time, I took the offer as a personal challenge, without having a sense of the actual adjustments that lay ahead: learning to work with a diverse constituency of more than two hundred students, a sometimes divergent faculty, and a new administrative bureaucracy, not to mention hundreds of members of the influential Garden Club of Georgia. While contemplating the move, I also considered the looming costs of college tuition for my two sons. The 50 percent salary increase associated with the offer became a deciding factor. And so it came to pass that I would smell the sweet scent of southern magnolias on the historic North Campus of the University of Georgia each spring for the next twenty-two years.

5

SOUTHERN ODYSSEY

For my first nine years at Georgia, I was dean of the School of Environmental Design, with an office on the top floor of Caldwell Hall, a contemporary building with wall-to-wall windows overlooking the historic campus six stories below. Dawna, Scott, and I lived in a pretentious French provincial house on St. George Drive rented from a faculty member who was on leave that year. (Jon had entered the University of Wisconsin–Madison when we moved south.) We were feted with numerous "Welcome to Georgia" events, including receptions at the Greek Revival mansion on Prince Avenue that was the home of the university president. Fairly quickly, I developed the ability to hold a plate and a wine glass in one hand, while picking up hors d'oeuvres with the other and engaging in small talk about the Bulldogs' prospects for the upcoming football season.

The two decades in Georgia were not all magnolias, crowded lecture halls, and social events. My parents, my brother Eldon, and his daughter Lisa all died during these years and my marriage crumbled. By 1985, I found myself a single parent to twelve-year-old Scott, and discovered that I could compensate, to some degree, for years of not giving enough time to my sons.

While the stint as dean brought with it a certain amount of stress, as any midlevel administrative position would, I tried to maintain a positive outlook and to encourage faculty members with handwritten notes acknowledging their achievements, among other deanly motivational practices. My real salvation from the trying aspects of academic administration was the decision to build a life outside of my role as dean, to spend more time with Scott, and to continue teaching both undergraduate and graduate courses. During my first semester at Georgia, I taught the woody plants course and learned about southern trees and shrubs alongside my sophomore students. While this was still a traditional course, I emphasized native species and began to relate them to the natural plant communities of Piedmont Georgia, the surrounding physiographic region. My subsequent courses in planting design nudged undergraduates to expand beyond liriope and English ivy as groundcovers by considering ferns, wildflowers, and even native grasses in their designs. In this first year, I collaborated with Sam Jones, a taxonomist in the botany department, on the development of a new lecture/lab course, Native Plant Communities of the Southeast, which we co-taught in the fall of 1984. Inspired by my experience teaching about Wisconsin plant communities with Evelyn Howell, this course also had its origins in the pioneering collaboration of Edith Roberts and Elsa Rehmann. Science met art once again.

After Sam and I launched the lecture/lab course, we initiated a field course

Gray's lilies on Black Balsam Knob, Pisgah National Forest, NC. Photograph by Darrel Morrison.

Mountain hairgrass and mountain oatgrass on Black Balsam Knob, Pisgah National Forest, NC. Photograph by Darrel Morrison.

in Georgia's three-week "Maymester" session the next spring. As I learned about southern plants and ecology from Sam, I began to admire these diverse, resilient, and beautiful native plant communities. For a time, I felt something akin to guilt for being unfaithful to my first love, the Wisconsin prairie, but soon recognized the similarities shared by native landscapes in the Midwest and the Southeast. For example, the grassy balds in the Smoky Mountains of North Carolina and Tennessee were open to the sky and the clouds, with grasses and sedges that waved in that wind, ocean-like, to the horizon. My favorite grassy bald for class field trips became the Black Balsam Knob along the Blue Ridge Parkway in North Carolina. Rising more than six thousand feet in elevation, the Knob is home to mountain hairgrass and mountain oat-grass, a fine-textured matrix punctuated in summer with the blue of dimin-

Heggie's Rock granite outcrop, Appling, GA. Photograph by Alan Cressler.

utive bluets, the orange of Gray's lilies, the chartreuse-green of hay-scented fern fronds, and the orange of an occasional flame azalea in bloom. Like the prairie, a grassy bald evokes a sense of freedom and vulnerability—exposure to rain, wind, and lightning. On one occasion the line of students following me to the top of Black Balsam Knob broke into the heroic chorus of "Climb Every Mountain," as I briefly became Baron von Trapp.

My favorite plant association in the Piedmont region of Georgia was the granite outcrop community, historically plentiful but now threatened. Most had succumbed to quarrying operations and ATV racetracks or were used as dumping grounds. A remarkable exception was Heggie's Rock, designated as a National Natural Landmark in 1980. The 101-acre site owned and managed by The Nature Conservancy is largely an open sunlit community, with expanses of dark gray rock, or gray streaked with pinkish to rust-colored tones, covered in patches of brown to emerald-green mosses and silvery-gray to bluish-green lichens. Soil depth varies from none on the bare rock to shallow soils supporting broomsedge, along with drifts of yucca and plants such as the yellow-flowered Confederate daisy and purple-flowered dwarf blazing star blooming together in September. In somewhat deeper soil, shrubs like sparkleberry and various sumac species flourish, and islands of still deeper soil sustain dwarfed versions of blackjack, post, and Georgia oaks, along with red cedars and stunted loblolly and shortleaf pines. These woody species often partially enclose various-sized "rooms" within the overall complex. Ephemeral pools seasonally display their own suite of diminutive—and often rare and endangered—species. In early spring, patches of the tiny red-leafed elf orpine, or *Diamorpha smallii,* "ooze" over the shallow, gravelly zones surrounding the ephemeral pools, giving the landscape a striking abstract expressionist look.

Elf orpine in ephemeral pool, Heggie's Rock, Appling, GA. Photograph by Alan Cressler.

Longleaf pine forest. Photograph by Randy Browning, USFWS Southeast Region (CC-BY-2.0).

In the Coastal Plain, I came to love the longleaf pine savannas, particularly those at Greenwood Plantation, a 4,000-acre tract in southwest Georgia, just outside Thomasville. Here, a 700-acre stand of old-growth longleafs known as the Big Woods provides a reminder that there were once 92 million acres of longleaf-dominated landscapes in nine southeastern states. Less than 0.01 percent of old-growth longleaf remains, a figure similar to the amount of original tallgrass prairie remaining in the state of Iowa.

On the first of August 2001, I spent an unforgettable twenty-four hours in the Big Woods with my dog Zeus. I had brought classes here many times before, but this visit was a special gift to me, granted by the Greentree Foundation, then the owner of the property. It was awe-inspiring to know that some of the longleafs swaying gently above our little one-man–one-dog tent were more than four hundred years old. They would have been two centuries old when Beethoven wrote his Fifth Symphony. The straight-trunked pines in the Big Woods may be as close as five feet or as distant as eighty feet apart. Beneath them is a luxuriant cover of varied grasses, with the fine-bladed wiregrass as the lead species. A collection of forbs—broad-leaved flowering plants

Species-rich ground layer in the Big Woods, Greenwood Plantation, GA. Photograph by Darrel Morrison.

Cumberland Island saltmarsh.

with jewel-toned flowers—mingles among the grasses. With twenty or more species growing in a single square meter, this plant community is the most diverse of any in the Southeast. From early spring to late fall, an ever-changing array of color flecks drifts through the grasses. "Flecks" is the key here, as dots of color constitute perhaps 5 percent of the scene at any one time. This is a lesson in the dramatic potential of subtlety. Lacking intense, solid color extravaganzas—like those provided by a mass of one showy species—the long-leaf pine community displays a "relay" of changing color flecks in the matrix of fine-textured grasses. Lying in the little tent in the Big Woods that night with Zeus at my feet, and the sound of an ever-so-gentle adagio of wind in the pines above, I felt tears running down my cheeks. My emotion reflected sadness over what we have lost, as well as the joy of knowing that these woods are still here, thanks to the foresightedness of people who continue to protect them.

The saltmarsh is at the other end of the diversity spectrum in southeastern landscapes. I was introduced to the regional saltmarsh while driving along Highway 17, a coastal route in Georgia and South Carolina where the roadway sometimes flies above the marshes on sleek concrete bridges. After sunset, I looked down from those bridges onto blackish saltmarshes with sinuous silver creeks snaking through them, reflecting the afterglow in the sky. Later, on May mornings aboard the *Cumberland Queen* en route to Cumberland Island with my field classes, the saltmarshes were vivid green bands of salt cordgrass between a leaden sky and dark water. In those field classes, and on Sapelo Island and along the Crooked River in Georgia, my students and I painted watercolors of saltmarshes. With the memory of expanses of waving grasses under an open Wisconsin sky still etched on my mind, I became smitten by their broad horizontal expanses. The overwhelmingly dominant species in these wetlands is salt cordgrass, *Spartina alterniflora,* a cousin of the northern prairie cordgrass, *Spartina pectinata,* the water-repellant ripgut grass we cut in the slough to cover our haystacks.

Meandering interior channels, or creeks, flow through the expansive saltmarshes, along which nutrients are deposited. The salt cordgrass growing alongside these enriched channels is tall and darker green, and this contrast with the less-nourished grasses leads to the fluid patterns reflecting the slow-moving streams. On the slightly higher ground adjacent to saltmarshes, there may be zones of the short, thin-bladed saltmeadow cordgrass, and black needlegrass, which is actually a rush. In the next-higher zone, there are salt-tolerant shrubs such as marsh elder and groundsel tree. As elevation increases, these give way to a forest dominated by picturesque evergreen live oaks, often draped in silver-gray Spanish moss. Beneath that canopy are patches of dramatic saw palmettos with spiky fanlike leaves. Where breaks in the canopy allow for more sunlight, there may be islands of broomsedge or bright green dogfennel, soft and feathery, moving in the slightest breeze. Where the salt-marsh grades into forest, there is a sense of order, with each plant species matched to its unique microenvironment.

The Okefenokee Swamp, at the far southeastern corner of Georgia, is another place I came to associate with my beloved prairie. FDR had the foresight to designate this 400,000-acre primordial landscape as a national wildlife preserve at the height of the Depression, in 1937, the year of my birth. I was surprised to learn of broad expanses called "prairies" in the Okefenokee Swamp complex but soon discovered that these resemble the tallgrass prairies of the Midwest only in horizontal expanse and openness to the sky. My students and

Chesser Prairie, Okefenokee Swamp, GA. Photograph by Peter May.

I experienced these prairies from canoes as we paddled through the sinuous, tannin-stained waterways. The dominant species is the waterlily, and in June and July, its fragrant white multipetaled flowers float among the leaves, elegant and refined and perfect. Where the water is shallower there are clumps of the upright leaves of goldenclub or "never-wet," so named because the leaves, if pushed under water, will come up dry, with water drops rolling off the surface. We saw small floating islands of yellow-green sphagnum moss, called "batteries," where hooded pitcher plants, blue flag irises, and even wet-tolerant Andropogon species grew.

I fondly remember touring through the Okefenokee's Chesser Prairie and Grand Prairie, pulling up alongside a particular plant species and using my oar to point it out to students. We learned so much more this way than from studying photographs in books and had much more fun. One November, I went on a solo trip to the Okefenokee and was thrilled to hear the primordial sound of a male alligator bellowing, part of a courtship ritual: "GrrraughhHHH!" During the following summer's field course, I promised the class that, in the spirit of the swamp, I would do the bellow for them. Once we were well into Chesser Prairie, I made good on my promise, starting with the low guttural sound and then crescendoing. It was flattering to hear other bellows approaching our cluster of canoes, but I was relieved that none of the guys coming toward us challenged me to a duel.

Before too long, I got over my guilt about being seduced by so many southeastern landscapes and became ever more appreciative of the people who have had a role in preserving and protecting wild landscapes. These include not only presidents, like Teddy and Franklin Roosevelt and Jimmy Carter, but also dedicated individuals at many levels of government, as well as nongovernmental agencies such as The Nature Conservancy and a growing number of other land conservancies across the country. We are indebted to everyone who has played a role in protecting threatened natural areas. These remarkable reserves are not only the province of natural diversity and biotic richness but also sources of great beauty—the beauty of the wild—which inspires and sustains us.

Back in Athens, I had been looking for a retreat-like home within commuting distance from town, and one Saturday morning in spring 1986, I came across a classified ad in the local paper for a five-acre site on the Oconee River.

Oconee River, near Athens, GA. Photograph by Darrel Morrison.

I arranged to meet the owner at the land that same morning. Driving out Barnett Shoals Road, I turned down a narrow winding driveway and entered a landscape of scraggly wild blackberries and small, closely spaced loblolly pines, growing where a cotton field probably existed fifty years earlier. Farther down the drive were more mature loblollies as well as a variety of oaks and hickories, with flowering dogwoods and young beeches under their canopy. On one side of the driveway, the ground dropped down to a small creek, the western boundary of the lot, which wound its way down to the Oconee River, the northern boundary.

I met the owner near the river, at an opening in the woods that probably resulted from a previous building effort that, for whatever reason, had gone awry. He led me down a narrow winding path toward the south bank of the river, with a view of the broad Oconee curving around a sandbar on the opposite shoreline. On "my" side of the river (I had already mentally taken possession of the lot by now), there was a rocky north-facing slope with a rich ground layer of woodland wildflowers and an old double-trunk beech tree (replete with initials carved into its trunk) clinging to the rocky slope. At the river's edge, gigantic granite boulders sloped down into the less-than-crystal-clear water. This was not a pristine, untouched landscape, but by now I was smitten with this little piece of Georgia, with all its history of human use and abuse.

With uncharacteristic restraint, I didn't immediately make an offer on the property. Scott and I returned each of the next three days, and when we finally decided to purchase it, my offer was accepted without any haggling. Within months, builder and friend George Wright completed our full-time residence, a twenty-by-twenty-four-foot cabin with a loft above the kitchen. It was gray clapboard, with muted blue trim and a tin roof. It had a wood deck along the east face, and an opening in the loblolly pines growing to the east let in the morning sunlight. Second- or third-growth mixed forest immediately surrounded the other three sides of the cabin, and large casement windows opened out into the woods, inviting them in.

Morrison's cabin on the Oconee, near Athens, GA. Photograph by Darrel Morrison.

Morrison's dog Zeus on a walk in the woods, near Athens, GA. Photograph by Darrel Morrison.

The next four years were good ones in many ways. On Sunday mornings, Scott, Zeus, and I went for walks in the five acres of woods, looking for the first hepatica flowering at the base of the old beech down near the river (as early as January some years) or for the delicately scented Piedmont azaleas and fringe tree that flower together on the riverbank in April and May. We often canoed on the river on Sunday afternoons, going upstream first, then making the easy trip back with the current. We were not recluses by any means. The *New York Times* was delivered to our mailbox, up the driveway on the road, each day. During the week, while I was teaching and administering, Scott was studying, pole-vaulting, and participating in various local theater productions. I followed in his footsteps, and when he was a senior, both of us landed roles in Town & Gown Players' *You Can't Take It with You*.

During Scott's New York college years, I frequently visited on weekends, flying into LaGuardia from Atlanta on Friday nights and returning to the tin-roofed cabin on Sunday nights. From his apartment in the Village, we often walked along the Hudson River and took the subway to Central Park, the Guggenheim, and the Metropolitan Museum. Whenever possible, we indulged our shared passion for theater and music by attending performances on Broadway and at the Metropolitan Opera.

Back home in Athens, the site of my earlier acting experience in the Town & Gown Players, I continued to audition for roles in local productions. I always felt most creative as a teacher and designer while involved in theater performances. Being on stage is a risk-taking, life-on-the-edge experience. What is my next cue? Will I remember my next line? I think that perhaps the mental stimulation of memorizing those lines and taking on a new persona on stage crossed over into both my designing and my teaching performance.

At this point in my life, I also came to appreciate the connection between music and design and the ways music can generate spontaneity and fluidity in a landscape architect's early design concepts. This was not my revolutionary discovery. In *Siftings*, Jensen tells the story of an employee in his office who was charged with the design and construction of a small stream and waterfall in Chicago's Humboldt Park Conservatory. The young man was having difficulty evoking the qualities he desired in his design. Jensen suggested he go home one evening and have his wife play Mendelssohn's "Spring Song" as inspiration. He thought Jensen was going daffy from overwork but went ahead and followed this advice. After repeatedly listening to the music, he struck just the right chord in his concept for the stream and waterfall.

In the mid-1980s, I began to use music in my own design work, playing different types of music appropriate to the project at hand. I let Philip Glass's "Low" Symphony guide me toward a design for the Martin Luther King Jr. Memorial competition. The tension in Glass's "Some Are" movement in that symphony helped me come up with a design that attempted to portray Dr. King's struggles en route to the passage of the Civil Rights Act and then the resolution that came with his "mountaintop" speech. I didn't win the competition, but I enjoyed the creative process.

In my undergraduate planting design classes and graduate garden design studio, I began to ask students for quick conceptual design studies, often multiple concepts for one site, inspired by music. After demonstrating the method, I encouraged the students to experiment with the technique, using chalk pastels on multiple overlays of their site plans. Rather than ambient background music, I chose dramatic pieces: the "Low" Symphony; the "Love" movement from George Duke's *Muir Woods Suite;* the aria "Nessun Dorma" from

Puccini's *Turandot;* "My Heart at Thy Sweet Voice" from Saint-Saëns's *Samson and Delilah;* and selections from an album of jazz that had inspired Jackson Pollack as he painted. My favorite piece for design inspiration remained *The Moldau,* Bedřich Smetana's portrayal of the river flowing through Czechoslovakia, the composition that had so moved me as a college freshman. One workshop, Designing with Music, that I led at the University of São Paulo was made special when my friend and colleague Catharina Lima persuaded her pianist son to perform live for the occasion.

As dean of the School of Environmental Design, one of my most enjoyable duties was hosting and preparing dinners in honor of visiting lecturers. With these occasions in mind, I asked George Wright to expand the tin-roofed cabin to include a dining room with seating for twelve and casement windows all along the north and south walls. Over the years, the dinners in the cabin provided not only fellowship but also insight into new design methods, new perspectives on landscape, and even cutting-edge ecological concepts. On one memorable occasion, I had the honor of hosting A. E. Bye. He sat on my left at dinner and, during the soup course, caught a glimpse of a dogfennel plant outside, its feathery-fine leaves waving in the breeze. Stopping short, spoon in midair, he asked, "Where did you get that *wonderful* plant?" I said something about it coming to my rumpled front garden of its own accord, and that my role lay simply in not removing it since I liked the way it moved. I felt we were kindred spirits from then on.

The dinners gave me opportunities to meet many accomplished practitioners and scholars from abroad as well, including the British geographer Jay Appleton, author of *The Experience of Landscape* (1975). Appleton's book advances his "prospect-refuge" theory, the idea that people have a preference for being in spaces where there is foreground enclosure (refuge), but with a long view, often into a sunlit opening (prospect). Fulfilling this human need became a concept I found worth striving for in my own designed landscapes.

Entertaining guest lecturers also gave faculty members at the University of Georgia the opportunity to become better acquainted outside of the university setting. I greatly admired the work of Eugene Odum, considered by many to be the father of modern ecology and founder of the University of Georgia Institute of Ecology. I invited him and his artist wife Martha to dinners at my house, where my design colleagues came to know them and personally to see links between science and art. Gene generously lectured in my undergraduate landscape ecology class, passing along his belief that the most exciting advances occur at the intersection of disciplines rather than within the boundaries of a single field. We were fortunate to have this humble, world-famous scientist bring such an important message to sophomores and juniors preparing to launch their careers.

The work of Rachel and Stephen Kaplan, environmental psychologists at the University of Michigan in Ann Arbor, made a significant impact on me during this period, but from a distance. The Kaplans' landmark book, *The Experience of Nature: A Psychological Perspective* (1989), epitomized the value of applying scientific research to the practice of landscape design. One of their studies indicated that people are most engaged by landscapes exhibiting four characteristics: mystery, complexity, coherence, and legibility. Mystery occurs in landscapes that are partially concealed, in other words, where there is always more to discover "around the bend." Complexity is derived from a diversity of forms, colors, and textures, which in landscapes often reflect species diversity. Coherence is perceived through patterns in the landscape—the "drifts" of different species based on microenvironmental differences or the ways plants reproduce. Legibility results when people are able to "read" how to move through a landscape without feeling claustrophobic or disoriented. I found the four characteristics useful for evaluating designs, and "mystery–complexity–coherence–legibility" became a bit of a mantra for me, both as a teacher and as a practitioner.

In 1990, I met Roberto Burle Marx, one of my most admired landscape design heroes, when he gave a lecture at Georgia Tech in Atlanta. As he talked about his work, I recalled my parents' Christmas gift of P. M. Bardi's book *The Tropical Gardens of Burle Marx*. After the lecture I introduced myself to him, and he responded with open arms, literally, imploring, "You *must* come to Brazil! We will have a party!" I was exhilarated at the thought of attending one of Marx's famed parties at the Sítio, his home in Guaratiba, outside Rio, but the trip seemed too costly, in both time and expense. After Marx's death four years later, I deeply regretted declining the invitation.

My first opportunity to begin a new project came in 1991, when I joined a team, headed by my colleague and longtime friend Ian Firth, to develop a restoration plan for the National Park Service's Manassas National Battlefield

View at the National Wildflower Research Center, Austin, TX. Photograph by Carol Betsch.

Park in Virginia. Restoration of the historic pattern of woodlands, grasslands, and fields existing in 1862 was a central element of the project. We developed a plan incorporating a patchwork of vegetative cover—a visual representation of the historic landscape that could also enhance wildlife habitat. After many delays, the Park Service implemented the plan in 2003.

Late in the fall of 1991, David Northington, executive director of the National Wildflower Research Center (NWRC) in Austin, Texas, invited me to be the senior member of a planning and design team for the center's proposed new headquarters on the southern edge of Austin. The complex was supported by Lady Bird Johnson, who donated the forty-two-acre site. I had first met David and Mrs. Johnson after making a presentation at the annual NWRC conference in Austin that spring. My previous experience working on her highway beautification projects in Washington, DC, twenty-five years earlier added to my interest in another Lady Bird project that would broadly promote the use of native plant community representations in designed landscapes. Besides David, who in addition to directing the NWRC held an appointment in the botany department at the University of Texas, the design team included two local landscape architects, Bob Anderson and Eleanor McKinney, and the architects Rick Archer and Bob Shemwell of Overland Partners in San Antonio. We would be starting from scratch, siting a cluster of buildings, driveways, parking areas, and trails, along with a complex of gardens and courtyards.

In early February 1992, I made my initial visit to the site—a combination

Texas live oaks and Ashe junipers, National Wildlife Research Center, Austin, TX. Photograph by Carol Betsch.

Site sketch by Morrison, National Wildlife Research Center, Austin, TX.

of formerly grazed land, prairies, and savannas with Texas live oaks and Ashe junipers. The subtly rolling topography was divided by a stream that became a broad river during heavy rains. On my first day, David and I walked the forty-two acres, getting an overview of the existing plant communities, botanizing, and discussing the ecological issues relevant to the landscape. Later that afternoon, I tried to capture the essence of the site through some watercolor sketches.

That night, I borrowed a tent and sleeping bag from David and camped on the site. Once the sun went down, the night came alive with sounds and smells: the cedar aroma from the Ashe junipers, and then at dawn, the morning birdsongs. The experience gave me a deeper sense of the place. After my first day on the building site, I went on more field forays with David into the surrounding Hill Country, all the while learning more about the land and about Texas plants. During the design process, the landscape architects worked directly with the building architects in a rewarding collaboration.

When I took on the deanship at Georgia, I saw myself in that role for no more than ten years, both for my own good and for that of the school. In 1992, I "stepped down," as academics like to say, but felt as if the change was actually a step up. Now I had the time and energy to devote to teaching the first-year graduate garden design studio, where I could merge ecology with art and music; to continue teaching both the lecture course and field course on native plant communities of the Southeast; and to take on more comprehensive design, management, and restoration projects.

My first new project after leaving the dean's office presented itself in 1993, when the Atlanta History Center asked me to develop a planting scheme for the area surrounding a new thirty-thousand-square-foot museum building designed by the prominent Atlanta architect George T. Heery. Not surprisingly, the landscape theme was a series of representations of native Georgia Piedmont plant communities, from an early-successional loblolly pine forest to a mid-successional pine-hardwood forest to a low streamside zone. I hired my former graduate student Gary Gullatte to assist me in the production of drawings for the project.

Behind the new museum building, a preexisting garden had been planted in an old granite quarry. Heery planned a granite cobblestone parking and entrance court with a curbed circular planting area centered in front of the new building. The history of granite quarrying on the site, in combination with the hot, sun-washed environment within the thirty-four-foot-diameter circle, suggested that this would provide a perfect opportunity to create a granite outcrop garden. Capturing the essence of a granite outcrop provided a challenging design problem, which I relished. I mulled over the form it should take, pulling out a sketch pad in spare moments and playing with the possibilities, but nothing clicked. Then, on a flight home from Prague, after a complimentary glass or two of wine, I spread my cocktail napkin out on my tray and sketched a blank circle. From there, a spiral form emerged, a large comma that could be a stylized ephemeral pool. An arc of a wall formed on one side of the circle, and a small tree appeared, off-center in the design. Openings between granite paving stones provided niches filled with lichens, mosses, and other diminutive plants I had seen at Heggie's Rock. With a bit of refinement, the arc of the low wall became a rising-and-falling arc, and the small tree became a Georgia oak, an endemic granite outcrop species.

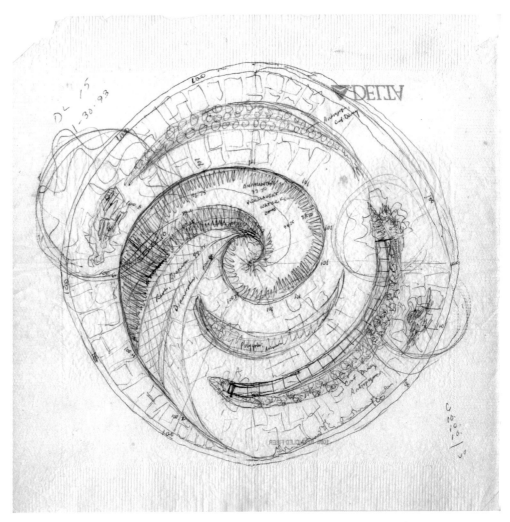

Concept sketch by Morrison, granite outcrop garden, Atlanta History Center, Atlanta, GA.

The final design was realized in collaboration with Thomas Rice and Rodney Clemons, two very talented Atlanta stonemasons. Their painstaking work and particularly sensitive execution of the rising and falling granite slab wall were crucial to the success of the project. The three of us picked flat paving stones from a stone scrap pile in a granite quarry south of Atlanta. We then carried out a plant rescue mission of sorts, collecting doomed lichens and mosses to place in the interstices between stones and selecting a gnarled Georgia oak, eight feet tall and at least that broad, from a soon-

Granite outcrop garden with Georgia oak, Atlanta History Center, Atlanta, GA. Courtesy Atlanta History Center.

to-be excavated zone. Thomas and Rodney carefully extricated the oak and hauled it to its new home. We planted it during a gentle rain less than two hours later and placed granite sand in the ephemeral pool bottom and as a bed for the plants growing between the flagstones. The next year sand cress and Confederate daisies spontaneously appeared, an unplanned bonus in the seedbank within our harvested granite sand. While that little garden was later a casualty of a major building expansion project, to me it was worth doing because it demonstrated that the essence of a delicate, complex natural community can be created in a limited space within a highly urban context, bringing a taste of that community's beauty to people who would never experience it otherwise.

The University of Georgia didn't have a faculty sabbatical program per se, but it did provide administrators who had stepped down an opportunity to do research or teach at another institution for a semester as a way of recharging. I availed myself of that perk in fall 1994, when I accepted an invitation to spend a semester teaching at the University of Michigan. I taught the introductory design studio for first-year graduate students in landscape architecture within the School of Natural Resources and Environment, most of whom had come with previous degrees in a wide spectrum of other disciplines. Throughout the semester, I was reminded of Eugene Odum's observation that the most interesting things emerge at the intersection of disciplines. We spent considerable time in the field, with forays into the restored prairie in the university's Nichols Arboretum and to natural forests, fens, and bogs both in southern Michigan and on the Upper Peninsula, where we also took a weekend field trip to the university's Biological Station. Sugar maples and beeches were at their peak fall color. At all of these sites, we laid out transects and quadrats to obtain quantitative data, identified and drew plants and sketched landscapes, and wrote about what we were seeing, hearing, and feeling.

I invited Rachel Kaplan to give a guest lecture to my class on human responses to natural environments. She accepted on the condition that I simultaneously illustrate it with sketches on the chalkboard. Afterward, we joked about taking "Mystery, Complexity, Coherence, and Legibility" on the road as the "Rachel and Darrel" show. It was an honor and a pleasure to work with the coauthor of *The Experience of Nature*.

That semester, my students and I designed with music and "channeled" renowned landscape architects from the past and present—ranging from Jens Jensen and Ossian Cole Simonds to Angela Danadjieva and Martha Schwartz. When we toured Fair Lane, the Henry Ford estate Jensen designed in 1914, the students were well aware that we had the world's leading Jensen scholar in our midst. My former student Bob Grese was a professor in the university's landscape architecture department and author of *Jens Jensen: Maker of Natural Parks and Gardens*. Bob and I first met in 1980, when he was choosing a graduate program in landscape architecture. Fortunately for all of us, he enrolled at the University of Wisconsin–Madison and, as I had, reaped the benefits of learning from the early ecological restoration work at the UW Arboretum. In my classes, he discovered Jensen's legacy, and I encouraged him to write a proposal for a National Endowment for the Arts grant to do a study of Jensen's Lincoln Memorial Garden in Springfield, Illinois. He was awarded the grant, and his research into the fifty-year history of the garden and its continuing management became the subject of his master's thesis, which he built on to create his definitive work on Jensen, published in 1992. It has been particularly rewarding for me as a teacher to learn from Bob and his monumental contribution to the literature of landscape history.

Beginning in the mid-1990s, I became a regular visiting teacher at the Conway School of Landscape Design in western Massachusetts. Decades earlier, Walter Cudnohufsky, a University of Massachusetts faculty member, had told me about his dream of starting a small, private school of landscape design in the Hilltowns. I thought the plan audacious and unlikely, but Walt pulled it off, beginning in 1972, with funding from a combination of student tuition, gifts, and grants from clients for whom students provided design services. Walt directed the intensive ten-month graduate-level program for twenty years.

My introduction to the school occurred in 1994, at the invitation of Don Walker, who had succeeded Walt as director two years earlier. In the 1970s, Don had been a faculty member at the University of Illinois, and when he brought a class of landscape architecture students to Madison, I led them on a tour of my recent project for the CUNA Mutual Insurance Company. The landscape plan included native prairie sweeps influenced by forms in Burle

Marx's Brazilian landscapes. Don thought that Conway students would be particularly intrigued by my approach to design, with its combination of ecology and art. When I joined the ranks of visiting faculty members, my perspective was expanded through interactions with the exceptionally motivated people in this unique school. The Conway School field trips were always among the high points of the year for me. We loaded into vans and went to places such as High Ledges Wildlife Sanctuary near Shelburne Falls and The Nature Conservancy's Hawley Bog. Faculty members Mollie Babize and Ken Byrne hosted dinners, and there were potlucks at the school. We enjoyed pancake breakfasts at sugar shacks during the maple syrup season, and late evening beers and dart games at the Conway Inn.

The National Wildflower Research Center and Atlanta History Center projects were becoming established in 1995, when the National Park Service contacted me about consulting on a complex historic restoration initiative—developing recommendations for vegetation management on several earthworks dating back to the Revolutionary and Civil Wars. This project involved extensive fieldwork at Fredericksburg & Spotsylvania National Military Park and Petersburg and Richmond National Battlefield Parks in Virginia; Stones River National Battlefield in Tennessee; and Ninety Six National Historic Site in South Carolina. I hired Kevin Risk, a graduate student in historic preservation, to assist me during the summer of 1995. We undertook an extensive vegetation sampling exercise on the earthworks sites to determine species cover and diversity, presence of invasive species, erosion or compaction, and aesthetic character. Kevin's meticulous notes provided the basis for developing management goals and objectives, as well as specific vegetation management practices for a cross section of case study sites. These were later incorporated into the NPS publication *Guide to Sustainable Earthworks Management*.[1]

In April 1995, a couple of months after the grand opening of the Texas complex, I taught Designing for Place, a two-week course at the new Wildflower Center, which incorporated field trips to many of the natural areas David and I had explored when he was teaching me about the Hill Country landscape. During the weekend overnight between the two weeks, at Lady Bird Johnson's invitation I stayed at the LBJ Ranch. Now a National Historical Park, the ranch is in the heart of the Hill Country, about sixty miles west of Austin and the Wildflower Center. There are rangelands for cattle, and around the historic house and surrounding buildings, native live oaks and various ornamental plantings. On Saturday afternoon, I made a watercolor sketch of an old live oak and gave it to Mrs. Johnson later that evening as a bit of a thank-you for her hospitality. She was her gracious self, thanking me and then recalling, "Somebody else gave me a painting when we had him here for dinner." After this rare lapse of memory, she turned to her daughter and asked, "Who was that, Luci?" To which she replied, "Mother, that was Marc Chagall."

Several years later, I was invited to a big gathering at an NWRC board member's house in Austin. Mrs. Johnson was receiving guests at the reception, and I lined up with others to greet her. She had suffered a stroke and her eyesight was poor, so I doubted she would recognize me. When it was my turn, I began with something like, "You may remember me, Mrs. Johnson. I'm Darrel Morrison." To which she responded, "*Of course* I remember you, Darrel. I tell all my friends how you slept on the land."

6

EXPANDING HORIZONS

Among the guests at the Wildflower Center's grand opening was David Collens, director of Storm King Art Center, a museum and five-hundred-acre outdoor sculpture park in Mountainville, New York, an hour and a half north of Manhattan. When we met, he invited me to become involved in an effort to introduce native grasses into the landscape there. This was my first opportunity to establish grasslands in the eastern United States. I knew that there had once been extensive grasslands in the East—the Hempstead Plains on Long Island, for example, forty thousand acres of prairie with many similarities to the tall grass prairie of the Midwest. So I relished the opportunity to work with many species I knew, along with some unfamiliar ones. I also looked forward to working with David, an exuberant leader who was also the curator of the collection, as well as with the landscape architect William A. Rutherford Sr.

In August 1996, I traveled from Georgia for my first of many visits to Storm King, located about four miles west of Storm King Mountain, which overlooks the Hudson River at the northern narrows of the Hudson Highlands. From the entrance, I drove up the main drive through an allée of sugar maples, past Alexander Calder's monumental black metal sculpture *The Arch* on the left and Robert Grosvenor's low, horizontal black metal bridge-like sculpture, *Untitled*, on the open field to the right. Beyond that was a composition of gigantic orange metal cylinders, Alexander Liberman's *Iliad*, and, in a flat plain to the

Islands of big bluestem, Canada wildrye, and Indiangrass with Alexander Liberman's *Adam* (1970), Storm King Art Center. © 2020 The Alexander Liberman Trust. Photograph by Jerry L. Thompson. Courtesy Storm King Art Center.

left, Tal Streeter's playful red vertical zigzag *Endless Column.* I continued on as the driveway curved up Museum Hill, with a fifty-year-old planting of pines with pole-like trunks on my right, and Kenneth Snelson's *Free Ride Home,* a composition of aluminum tubes with stainless steel cable, down a slope to my left. At the top of the hill, I arrived at a Normandy-style chateau built in 1935, now both a museum and the administrative building for the art center.

Storm King had been founded in 1960 by Ralph E. Ogden and H. Peter Stern as a museum for Hudson River School painting, but by the following year both had decided to focus on modern sculpture. William A. Rutherford Sr., who had been involved in shaping the Storm King landscape from the beginning, once described the Art Center as "one big overall sculpture into which you add other sculptures." As David and Bill explained at our first meeting, the proposed effort to establish large sweeps of native tall grasses to contrast with broad curving "rivers" of mown turfgrass had the potential to reinforce, and even intensify, the concept of Storm King as "one big overall sculpture." Although captivated by the prospect of working toward that ambitious goal, I cautioned that it wouldn't be quick and it wouldn't be easy.

On our initial tour of the site that day, I noted that non-native weed species thrived in all sunny areas that were not regularly mowed. We would be fighting a battle with spotted knapweed in dry areas and purple loosestrife in wet, poorly drained ones. From my experience on the farm, I knew that weeds seemed to be suppressed in areas planted in the perennial forage crop, alfalfa, for two or more years. Instead of plunging into a program of planting native grass mixes the next spring, I recommended seeding cover crops as "placeholders," and native grasses later. In spring 1997, upland sites would be

Peninsulas of native grasses in South Fields with Mark di Suvero's *Pyramidian* (1987/1998) and *Beethoven's Quartet* (2003), **Storm King Art Center.** *Pyramidian*, gift of the Ralph E. Odgen Foundation; *Beethoven's Quartet*, courtesy Tippet Rise Art Center. © Mark di Suvero, courtesy the artist and Spacetime C.C. Photograph by Jerry L. Thompson. Courtesy Storm King Art Center.

planted with annual oats and perennial alfalfa. Although ocean-like waves of native grasses would not appear that year, quick-to-germinate bluish-green waves of oats would become two-and-a-half-feet-tall golden waves by mid-July, when they could be cut and baled. Beneath the oats crop, dark green perennial alfalfa would soon grow to two feet, contrasting with the broad mown pathways both in color and in texture. And by September, the alfalfa could be cut and baled for the first time. A perennial, it would be back next year, without the oats. Each of the next few summers, the alfalfa could be cut and baled two to three times, with the bales serving as pieces of sculpture in the fields until they were picked up for use as cattle food. Meanwhile, in the flat, low-lying field to the left of the main entrance driveway, we planted buckwheat as a cover crop, known for its ability to outcompete many weed species.

Shortly before becoming immersed in the Storm King project, I had re-

Drifts of switchgrass at the Forest edge, near Andy Goldsworthy's *Storm King Wall* (1997–98), Storm King Art Center. © Andy Goldsworthy, courtesy Galerie Lelong & Co., New York. Photograph by Jerry L. Thompson. Courtesy Storm King Art Center.

Tallgrasses in fall color with Richard Serra's *Schunnemunk Fork* (1990–91), Storm King Art Center. © 2020 Richard Serra/Artists Rights Society (ARS), New York. Photograph by Jerry L. Thompson. Courtesy Storm King Art Center.

ceived an invitation from Penn State to deliver the John R. Bracken Lecture and to accept the university's annual Bracken Medal in spring 1996. I couldn't imagine a higher honor. Although I had never met John Bracken, I felt that I knew him through his students, Joe Kondis and Frank Kemple, my colleagues who had passed on his teachings at the planning office in Maryland. The design philosophy I developed as a young professional was shaped by Bracken's ecological approach to landscape architecture, and I felt indebted to him for forging a path that made so much sense, in terms of both ecology and human needs. Bracken had similarly inspired his student A. E. Bye, the Bracken Medal recipient six years earlier.

In 1996, too, I was invited to write a foreword to the reprint edition of Roberts and Rehmann's *American Plants for American Gardens,* the book that was so fundamental to my education as a designer and a teacher. It was a great pleasure to be part of the University of Georgia Press's initiative to bring the 1929 book back into print, especially since the original edition had become relatively rare.

That fall, we took the first step in our battle to conquer invasive species and establish a meadow landscape at Storm King Art Center. After a single application of Rodeo, a glyphosate herbicide that was then considered to be safe, we planted a successful crop of buckwheat the following summer. It soon became clear that the upcoming work was essentially farming or, as Bill called it, "artistic farming," and he brought Bruce McCord, a local farmer, on board for that role. Bruce, with his wife Kim, was centrally involved in the planting and management aspects of the project for the next thirteen years. On my advice, the center purchased a Truax seed drill, a machine that greatly facilitated the planting of native grasses. In 1997, the program to plant a cover crop of oats and alfalfa was extended into large upland expanses through the midsection of the site. The next year, the low, poorly drained plain to the left of the entrance drive, home to Calder's *Arch* and Streeter's *Endless Column,* was planted in a mix of switchgrass, Indiangrass, and Canada wildrye to replace the previous crop of buckwheat.

In 1997, Gregory Armstrong, director of the UW Arboretum, called me in Georgia to discuss a project they were about to embark on which he knew would interest me: a native plant garden. It ultimately turned out to be my all-time favorite garden design project, in part because it afforded me a nostalgic look into my professional past. When, as a new graduate student in 1967, I first saw the Curtis Prairie, I never imagined that I would have the opportunity, thirty years later, to design a native garden overlooking that magnificent prairie restoration. But without realizing it, I had been preparing to design the Native Plant Garden during my many years of teaching field courses on native Wisconsin communities: prairies, savannas, forests, and fens.

The arboretum envisioned a native plant garden on four acres surrounding an expanded visitor center. My plan for it comprised a series of plant community vignettes, each of which is intended to capture the essence or "spirit" of the community it represents. While they cannot be considered true ecological restorations, they typically incorporate the dominant and the most abundant species in their community type as well as what I like to call "visual essence" species, those which exhibit distinctive visual characteristics that are indicators of that community. A good example is the prickly pear cactus in the sand prairie garden.

At the beginning of the project, I was given lists of species to include in each community type that arboretum scientists selected for representation. In many cases, these were derived from John Curtis's community summaries in *The Vegetation of Wisconsin,* supplemented by recent scientific literature and personal observation. Almost four hundred species were represented in the dozen plant communities. Having a master plant species list in hand be-

Aerial view, Native Plant Garden, University of Wisconsin–Madison Arboretum. Photograph by Bryce Richter / © Board of Regents of the University of Wisconsin System.

fore developing a plan put me in an unusual position as a designer. For some specialized community types, such as the sand prairie, limestone prairie, and wetland communities, the site would require manipulation: grading to change the topography and modify the soil composition.

During the summer of 1997, I spent time walking the site to get a feel for subtleties in the landscape which might suggest locations for specific plant community representations and to identify significant views. I also met with representatives of Friends of the Arboretum, the arboretum board, and staff members to learn their expectations for the new garden. Equipped with a site inventory and an understanding of programmatic needs, I developed an over-all mass:space plan for the four acres. This involved designation of the "mass," the tree canopy and zones of intermediate vegetation such as shrubs and tall

Conceptual plan by Morrison, Native Plant Garden, UW Arboretum. Photograph of plan by Robert Jaeger.

grasses. The "spaces" are zones of shorter vegetation, typically below eye level: lower shrubs and herbaceous planting, lawn areas, and pathways. The mass:space plan is an abstraction but is based on knowledge of the site and its potential uses. I like to work "fast and loose" at this stage of the game, with chalk pastels on overlays of the site plan.

During the past twenty years, I have often done mass:space concepts under the influence of music. For the Native Plant Garden, I listened to the flowing "Love" theme in George Duke's *Muir Woods Suite*. Duke was inspired by the ancient redwood forest in northern California, and it seemed appropriate to do a conceptual landscape design accompanied by a piece of music that had itself been motivated by a landscape. Duke probably knew that the woods were named for the renowned conservationist John Muir, but he may not have known that Muir was once a student at the University of Wisconsin. The concept plan that emerged from the design with music included broadly curving major walkways and mass:space relationships. In the final design, "masses" translated to forest and savanna representations: maple-basswood and oak-hickory forests; black oak and bur oak savanna; and a red cedar–birch composition. "Spaces" translated to non-canopied areas: a broad "river" of lawn flowing generally east-west through a central space to the north of the visitor center; curvilinear zones of prairie; and wetlands designed to capture and store rainwater runoff from the roof of the visitor center. All of the plant community representations in the Native Plant Garden are based on natural models in southern Wisconsin.

By manipulating the site, we were able to facilitate the development of a range of specialized habitats that otherwise could never have been experienced in one place. The land grading created water-collecting depressions, which became "homes" for fen, sedge meadows, and wet prairie communities, and the

Curtis Prairie overlook before the mesic prairie planting, Native Plant Garden, UW Arboretum, 2004.
Photograph by Susan Carpenter.

Curtis Prairie overlook eight years after planting, Native Plant Garden, UW Arboretum, 2012. Photograph by Susan Carpenter.

addition of limestone gravel allowed for a limestone prairie on the hillside at the southwest corner of the visitor center. This prairie, designed to resemble the dry prairie slopes of Iowa County, featured side-oats grama, little blue-stem, and prairie dropseed grasses, along with purple and white prairie clover, dyer's weed goldenrod, leadplant, prairie coreopsis, and sky-blue asters. On a warm slope to the south of the visitor center, the addition of a deep layer of sand made it possible to build a sand prairie. This landscape has anteced-ents in the sandy oak barrens near Mazomanie with its little bluestem, prairie Junegrass, lupines, prickly pear cactus, beardtongue, and dotted monarda or horsemint. The expansion of the visitor center itself led to the formation of new microhabitats: cool shaded zones on the north and warm reflective areas to the south and southwest sides of the expanded building.

The design included three communities based on regional forests. The maple-basswood forest drew on Abraham's Woods, a protected forest on a northeast-facing slope twenty-five miles south of Madison, where wild ginger, mayapple, multiple fern species, and spring ephemerals are at home. The oak-hickory forest representation was modeled after the composition of New Observatory Woods, an oak-hickory forest fifteen miles west of Madison, with its gray dogwood, hazelnut, and nannyberry shrub layer, and ground layer of wild geranium, woodland phlox, columbine, and Pennsylvania sedge. The red cedar–paper birch community at the western terminus of the river-like space to the north of the visitor center was inspired by a cedar glade at Lodde's Mill Bluff, overlooking the Wisconsin River near Sauk City.

Clockwise from top left: pale purple coneflower; spiderwort, prairie coreopsis, hoary vervain; prairie dropseed, heath aster; Pennsylvania sedge, spiderwort, prairie phlox. Photographs by Susan Carpenter.

Limestone prairie garden, Native Plant Garden, UW Arboretum, 2006. Photograph by Susan Carpenter.

Black oak savanna section, Native Plant Garden, UW Arboretum, 2006. Photograph by Susan Carpenter.

In 2003, Susan Carpenter, the garden's first curator, began a successful campaign to establish the Native Plant Garden as a foremost example of a designed ecological site. Along with dozens of dedicated volunteers motivated by her leadership, Susan has worked tirelessly on behalf of the garden. For both of us, one of the most rewarding aspects of the project has been knowing that thousands of schoolchildren see the landscape evolve each year when they visit on annual field trips. It was planted before they were born and must seem as if it evolved naturally. I like to think that it did.

In 1999, Scott and I finally made the trip to Rio. After visiting the Sítio, Burle Marx's home and garden, which now operates under the aegis of IPHAN, the National Institute of Historic and Artistic Heritage, we were treated to a meal at the nearby home/restaurant of César da Silva, who had

White sage in the mesic prairie section, Native Plant Garden, UW Arboretum. Photograph by Susan Carpenter.

been Marx's cook and nearly constant companion for a quarter century. At the end of the dinner, César gave me a copy of Laurence Fleming's book *Roberto Burle Marx: um retrato,* which he signed, "From Burle Marx' cook and very good friend, César." Over the next four years, I made four more trips to Brazil, two of which involved teaching in a program sponsored by the International Federation of Landscape Architects (IFLA) at the University of São Paulo.

By 2000, I had begun to think about where I might retire after my Georgia career. I was drawn back to Wisconsin, and since Jon and his family were in Madison, the nearby Driftless Area particularly attracted me. The last glacier that had smoothed out much of the state ten thousand years ago had bypassed this region, so the "drift" of stony rubble typically deposited during the gla-

Black oak savanna section, Native Plant Garden, UW Arboretum. Photograph by Susan Carpenter.

Prairie cordgrass with yellow coneflower in the wet-mesic prairie section, Native Plant Garden, UW Arboretum. Photograph by Susan Carpenter.

Long prairie vista with bluejoint grass in the wetland area, Native Plant Garden, UW Arboretum. Photograph by Susan Carpenter.

ciation process was not present. That year, I kept in touch with a realtor who was on the lookout for land that might interest me. After locating many properties with deal-breaking drawbacks, she finally sent photos of a twenty-acre parcel that seemed promising. Sixteen acres of the site were occupied by a rich hardwood forest on a steep north-facing slope, which extended over a ridge and partway down a south-facing slope, where paper birches and scattered red cedars feathered into a rocky dry prairie. As I studied the photographs from faraway Georgia, it was apparent that this was a high-quality natural prairie remnant with all the "right" colors of little bluestem, side-oats grama grass, northern prairie dropseed, and Indiangrass. Once again, I was seduced

View of cropland from the dry prairie slope, Driftless Area near Muscoda, WI. Photograph by Darrel Morrison.

by a beautiful landscape and made an offer. I soon found myself the owner of twenty acres in Wisconsin's Driftless Area near the small town of Muscoda.

In the meantime, while plant community "vignettes" were becoming established in the Native Plant Garden at the arboretum, tall grasses were becoming a part of the Storm King Art Center landscape in New York. By 2000, we began replacing the alfalfa plantings with native grass plantings in areas south of Museum Hill. The next year, I recommended that we introduce controlled burning into the management mix. Bruce and Kim McCord, with assistants, conducted the first burn in the low area to the north of the entrance drive in April 2002. By this time the grasses, and particularly the switchgrass, were thriving and were further stimulated by the burn. Purple loosestrife was now almost nonexistent in this area. The burns demonstrated why native North American people used fire as a major landscape management tool. The process promoted the growth of native warm-season grasses, added nutrients to the soil in usable form, suppressed cool-season exotic species and woody plants, and replaced dry stalks and leaf blades with fresh, green growth.

Over the next several years, whenever I returned to Madison for family visits, I drove the fifty miles out to the Iowa County land, sometimes clambering up the steep prairie slope with Jon. At other times I went alone, or with Zeus, and searched for a spot on the sloping prairie hillside that was flat enough to accommodate our little tent and slept there. If mosquitoes were not too abundant, I would just crawl into my sleeping bag and sleep under the stars. I imagined myself living on the land someday. But I still had places to go, and things to do, before that could happen.

During the 2002 Christmas vacation, Scott and I traveled to Manaus, Brazil, then on to an ecolodge in the Amazon rain forest, with a two-day stopover in Brasília. On this trip I visited many of Burle Marx's landscapes and met people who had worked with him, accompanied him on *coletas,* and sung boisterously at his Sítio parties. Now I admire Burle Marx not only for his work but, increasingly, for living his eighty-five years to the fullest.

The year 2003 was pivotal. In February, fourteen-year-old Zeus died, leaving me alone in the tin-roofed house on the Oconee River. At the end of spring semester, I had completed twenty years as a faculty member at the University of Georgia, which qualified me to retire with benefits. I decided to finish my career on a high note in 2004 by teaching the three-week Maymester field course that had meant so much to me. But first, during the summer of 2003, while Scott was away, I sublet his room and lived in New York on West 14th Street, with his two roommates. The timing was ideal. Life on the Oconee had become lonely. The idea of a two-month vacation in the big city before my final year of teaching was exciting.

That summer I made monthly visits to Storm King to monitor the tallgrass plantings. A major new planting was implemented in areas disturbed by regrading and construction of new driveways and a passenger elevator at the base of Museum Hill. Planted in June, the seed mix included little bluestem, Canada wildrye, Indiangrass, and partridge pea, an annual legume. The planting was one of the most weed-free of any we ever initiated. By the

Indiangrass, switchgrass, and big bluestem on Museum Hill, Storm King Art Center, with a partial view of David von Schlegell's *Untitled* (1972). © David von Schlegell. Photograph by Jerry L. Thompson. Courtesy Storm King Art Center.

next year it would be a grassland restorationist's dream, with the graceful arching seedheads swaying in the breeze and intermingling flecks of yellow partridge pea flowers.

In addition to a beginning acting class I registered for, my summer vacation was filled with trips to parks and gardens, including Michael van Valkenburgh's Teardrop Park and the Battery Park City complex. I loved venturing over to Gantry Plaza State Park at Hunter's Point in Queens and to the northern tip of Manhattan to Fort Tryon Park and the Cloisters, which had first entranced me on my initial visit to New York in 1959.

At the end of that rejuvenating summer, I left the bright lights of New York City and returned to the banks of the Oconee River for my final year on the Georgia faculty, concluding with the Southeastern Native Plant Communities field course in May. By then, I was teaching it with Nancy Aten, a former student at The Clearing in summer 1999. She had enrolled in the MLA program at Georgia in spring 2000 and took the Maymester field course that year. For the next four years, she was officially my teaching assistant but for all practical purposes my co-teacher—a model of energy, organization, and creativity. After The Clearing experience, she had plunged headlong into the world of "landscape design as ecological art."[2]

Afterward I made another trip to Brazil to teach in the IFLA program and see more of Burle Marx's work. My next stop was Logan, Utah, where I spent the fall semester as a visiting faculty member at Utah State University. My responsibilities included teaching the undergraduate planting design class and collaborating with the design and planning team in developing goals and objectives for the new USU Botanical Center in Kaysville.

Once again I faced a steep learning curve, with a whole new set of plants and plant communities to get to know, and once again I leaned on a scientist for support. Bill Varga of the USU plant science department literally guided me on multiple trips through the state's richly varied landscapes. We traveled eastward from Logan, up Logan Canyon to the meadows surrounding Tony Grove Lake in the Bear River Range. At higher than 8,000 feet, the meadow was punctuated with flecks of jewellike blooms: columbines, delphiniums, penstemons, and many more. We drove westward out of Logan, unloaded Bill's canoe from the top of his car, and put in at the Little Bear River landing. The adjacent wetlands were waterways with islands of emergent aquatic plants, a beautiful study in mass and space. Bill also introduced me to the geologic and botanic riches of Monument Valley, as well as Arches and Canyonlands National Parks near Moab.

The next fall, I returned to Utah State for the semester. During this second Utah gig, I teamed up with Bill, Susan Meyer, and Roger Kjelgren on a book titled *Landscaping on the New Frontier: Waterwise Design for the Intermountain West,* to which I contributed an introduction and a chapter on design, with a case study of a hypothetical suburban lot. In the introduction, I summarized my impressions of the Utah landscape:

> Big skies filled with dramatic clouds and magnificent sunsets . . . vast expanses of dry desert, monumental mountains, fantastic red rock formations and canyonlands that fade into a purple and blue infinity . . . meandering streams lined with red osier dogwoods, willows and cottonwoods that turn brilliant red and yellow in the fall . . . dry mountainsides blanketed with golden grasses, silver-green rabbitbrush and sage, dark dots of pinyon pine and juniper drifting down their steep faces; dense, dark spires of white fir covering north-facing slopes and cascading down drainageways . . . groves of gambel oaks with twisted trunks and branches blanketing lower slopes.

In a way I was channeling Elsa Rehmann, whose descriptions of native northeastern plant communities in *American Plants for American Gardens* helped awaken me to the sheer beauty of those landscapes. It seemed ironic, and sad, to me that people who were initially drawn to the natural beauty of Utah's native landscapes often replaced them with generic, irrigation-requiring landscapes, bereft of native vegetation and without a sense of where they were.

At the end of the semester, I drove east, watching the mountains to the west recede in my rearview mirror. After an overnight on the Oconee, I headed north to teach the undergraduate planting design class at Rutgers. Jean Marie Hartman, one of my students at Wisconsin in the 1970s, was now chair of the Rutgers landscape architecture program. Jean Marie introduced me to the Pine Barrens, a fascinating ecosystem in the New Jersey coastal plain. Over a million acres of the Pine Barrens had been designated as the Pinelands National Reserve in 1978. On our trips there, I saw plant species I had previously met in the sandhills of Georgia; others I had come to know in the bogs of northern Wisconsin; and still others that were new to me: pitch pine, sheep laurel, broom crowberry, and pyxie-moss. There are always new plants to meet.

By this time, I had begun to tire of my nomadic teaching schedule, which always involved saying goodbye to interesting people and places. At sixty-nine, I found myself considering options for settling down. One of the alternatives was building on my twenty acres of land in the Driftless Area. I envisioned a little house on the prairie—a small minimalist house, off the grid, tucked into the south-facing slope just below the hillside prairie. The south facade would be mostly glass, with long views across a valley framed by a couple of foreground oaks. Even as I fantasized about building my refuge (with its stunning prospect), both Jon and Scott encouraged me not to do it. They imagined me as a hermit who might easily trip and fall down the steep prairie slope, my body later discovered at the bottom of the hill. I took their advice to heart, reminding myself that I could still picnic and botanize on the land with family and friends during my trips to Madison. The other place that consumed my thoughts was a bit less bucolic. For three years New York had been my home for short stints, and now that I had a taste of it, I found myself enticed by the prospect of a more extended stay, a bit like many young people have done over the years. But instead of making the move as a youth, I made it as I approached seventy.

7

NEW YORK CITY DECADE

So, early in January 2006, I took the plunge into the maelstrom that is New York City. Since I would be commuting to New Brunswick to teach at Rutgers twice a week, I found an apartment in the Kips Bay neighborhood, a few blocks east of Penn Station. Walking in my new neighborhood, I began to recognize faces and others began to recognize me. I heard children playing in the school yard and musicians practicing in their apartments and got to know the professional dog walkers making their rounds with their charges. Over time, I became part of the place. As time passed I progressed from East 32nd Street to a sublet near Columbia to a studio on Riverside Drive. After a year there, I found a permanent home in a six-story co-op building on West 85th Street. I had sold the tin-roofed house in Georgia, making it possible to buy a four-hundred-square-foot apartment with windows all along the south wall, providing great views of the midtown Manhattan skyline, and sunlight and warmth on winter days. There I found warmth as well in neighbors who over time became my New York family and lifelong friends. During my decade of semiretirement on the Upper West Side, I was able to indulge my love of art and theater. It was just a quick walk across Central Park to the Met and the Guggenheim. I most remember the 2009 Kandinsky retrospective there, especially his circa 1914 work, so full of color, energy, and excitement. Another perk of living near Central Park was walking over to attend many wonderful

performances at Shakespeare in the Park. I also signed up for George Bartenieff's Shakespearean acting class, which taught me a lot about overcoming
inhibitions and taking risks and having fun, on stage and off. I knew I wasn't
quite ready for retirement, and in the fall of 2007, I began teaching planting
design in the Columbia University Master of Landscape Design program in
the School of Continuing Education and at the New York Botanical Garden.
When I first arrived in the city, I had met Charles Yurgalevitch, director of the
School of Professional Horticulture at NYBG. He facilitated my development
of a series of short courses on the design and management of woodlands and
woodland gardens, eastern meadows, and ecological landscapes.

On three occasions in the following years, NYBG asked me to teach a
field course at Black Rock Forest, a 3,870-acre tract in the western Hudson
Highlands established in 1929 by a local family as a research and education

Black Rock Forest, Hudson Highlands, NY. Photograph by Tom Doyle / *Park Connect* (NYS Office of Parks, Recreation and Historic Preservation).

Watercolor sketch by Morrison, Black Rock Forest, Hudson Highlands, NY, fall 2015.

resource. Now owned and managed by the Black Rock Forest Consortium, the forest is a rich complex of increasingly rare native plant communities ranging from wetlands and hardwood forest slopes to granite outcrops that emerge from seas of hay-scented ferns and rocky pinnacles where pitch pines cling to lichen- and moss-encrusted granite boulders. The forest has a history that includes centuries of human activity, but it still seems intact and wild. Although it's only a little more than an hour's drive from Manhattan, Black Rock Forest remains an incomparable reserve of natural diversity and beauty because of the consistent efforts of generous, visionary stewards. My courses at Black Rock not only reengaged me in teaching but also reconnected me with my design work—Storm King Art Center is almost next door.

It wasn't long before I found myself designing landscapes and gardens again. The first of these New York projects began in 2009, at New York University. I first learned about a plan for a native plant garden from George Reis, NYU's supervisor of sustainable landscaping. He had attended a talk I gave at Columbia during summer 2007 and asked if I would consider designing it. The tiny site came with many constraints, but I was intrigued by the prospect.

The history of Manhattan island grounded George's conception of the garden. On September 12, 1609, Henry Hudson had arrived in what is now known as New York Harbor on the island that the indigenous people called "Mannahatta" or "island of many hills." Hudson was hoping to discover a route to China but instead found an island inhabited by a rich array of plant and animal life as well as the Lenni Lenapi, who had lived there for a thousand years. Four centuries later, most of the native plant and animal life has been crowded out, replaced by buildings, paved surfaces, plants and animals from other continents, and a dense human population of over sixty-six thousand people per square mile.

To draw attention to the area's history, George advanced the idea of installing a "native woodland garden" in NYU's Schwartz Plaza, an area of 2,200 square feet on the east side of the library building, bounded by West 3rd Street on the south and West 4th on the north, across from Washington Square. George envisioned a garden that would commemorate Hudson's arrival in New York, featuring only plants that were believed to be living here then. The Native Woodland Garden was selected for the Class of 2008 gift and awarded $25,000 for its execution, with a target date of September 12, 2009, for its completion.

The boundaries of the garden were already established by the reddish-hued library on the west and a multiuse building housing the NYU visitor center on the east. In my design I had to consider how both of the buildings blocked the light, first in the morning and later in the afternoon, leaving a couple of midday hours of bright sunlight. In the course of designing the garden I realized that these constraints actually benefited the project. The garden would be seen by the thousands of people who pass through the space every day.

A system of rectilinear planters, a foot higher than the broad rectilinear walkway through the space, was a permanent feature of the site. The raised planter at the north end contained a shiny stainless steel abstract sculpture by Arthur Carter, as well as four non-native littleleaf linden trees whose dense canopies blocked most of the sunlight from that end of the garden. I asked George if there was any possibility of replacing the lindens with native trees that would not cast such deep shade. Upon reflection, we agreed that removing trees to create a woodland garden would not go over well with the public. The lindens lived on . . . for a while.

One of the main sources of information and inspiration for the design was Eric W. Sanderson's landmark book *Mannahatta: A Natural History of New York City*. A product of ten years' research, the book reveals the presence of fifty-five different ecosystems and reconstructs Mannahatta as it would likely have been four hundred years ago, when Hudson landed at New York Harbor. Sanderson's research includes a list of 627 plant and animal species that were probably on the island in 1609. Only a small percentage could have been growing on a one-twentieth-of-an-acre site like ours. I had no illusion that the Native Woodland Garden could reconstruct a piece of the historic Manhattan forest, but found the challenge of trying to capture the spirit of a native woodland in a limited urban space a compelling goal. Not only did I want to show it could be done, but more important, I wanted to give the people who experienced the garden each day a sense of the former botanical richness of the "island of many hills."

I drew on Sanderson's vast Mannahatta research to develop a list of plants—mainly native ground layer species—that were believed to have grown in the West Village vicinity. I narrowed the list to the approximately thirty-five species that seemed most likely to grow in the admittedly unnatural environment of Schwartz Plaza. Implementation of my plan began in spring 2009. I was on-site with George Reis and Matt Dubitsky, the NYU gardener who has nurtured the Native Woodland Garden from its beginning. After compost was worked into the soil, minor topographic variations were created with hand tools: subtle ridges oriented in a northwest-southeast direction. I then created drifts of herbaceous species reflecting the direction of the slight ridges. The ferns include Christmas, interrupted, hay-scented, and New York. Among the few dozen sedges were drifts of wild geranium, wild ginger, white wood aster, woodland phlox, wild columbine, mayapple, and blue-stemmed goldenrod.

The Native Woodland Garden has had its share of vicissitudes along the way. In addition to errant dogs tramping through, various construction projects required scaffolding that blocked the sunlight and compromised the planting beds. One project in 2010, however, proved fortuitous from my perspective. Construction of a major utilities tunnel through the north end of the garden necessitated the removal of the non-native littleleaf lindens and, with them, their dense shade. The next year, we planted a drift of seven native musclewood trees—whose canopies would be less dense—and replaced the drifts of ground layer plants that had succumbed to the excavation project.

According to Sanderson, musclewoods were likely growing in the neighborhood in 1609, and now, just over four hundred years later, those we planted on Schwartz Plaza are thriving. Matt Dubitsky noted that rhizomatous ground layer species—hay-scented fern, New York fern, white wood aster, wild ginger, blue-stemmed goldenrod, mayapple, and Solomon's seal—are also doing particularly well. The garden is used as an educational resource by NYU's Environmental Conservation Education program, and one of its graduates, Robert M. Clark, wrote a *Plant Field Guide* with a brief history of the garden accompanied by color photographs of selected species.[1] In the face of many challenges, George, Matt, and student volunteers brought a glimpse of Manhattan's botanical heritage to the West Village.

On a chilly gray December day in 2009, Todd Forrest, Gregory Long, and I stood under the canopy of two ancient sycamore trees and looked up a steep slope on the grounds of the New York Botanical Garden. The one-time P. Lorillard Snuff Mill, a beautiful three-story stone structure built in 1840, was on our left, and the Bronx River rushed downstream behind us. Todd, vice president of horticulture at NYBG, had invited me to do an informal slide presentation of my design work, to which he brought in Gregory, NYBG's president. Realizing that my work was not as obviously designed as many of the gardens at NYBG, I mentioned to Gregory that he might not see the design in my nature-inspired drifts. But he did.

Afterward, the three of us boarded a golf cart bound for the historic mill building. As we looked up the slope, Todd asked me if I might be interested in creating a design for the one-acre-plus site using native plants as my palette—which would be consistent with the LEED Silver Certification NYBG had earned with their restoration of the mill. Protection from erosion on the steep slope was a high priority. Views of the Old Stone Mill from the stone bridge crossing the Bronx River were important, as were views of that picturesque bridge from the large terrace behind the mill, the future venue for weddings and receptions. It would be primarily a viewing garden, since the steepness of the slope precluded pedestrian trails through it. A boulder-lined drainage channel to carry sometimes high volumes of stormwater was under construction in the southern part of the site. A stairway to provide river access for canoeists had been proposed, but the canoe landing was subsequently moved upstream, giving us more planting space. The date for the opening celebration of the restored mill—September 8, 2010—was less than nine months away, and Todd emphasized that making the landscape beautiful by then was my central assignment.

A month later, I met with Todd and his staff to discuss two preliminary design concepts. The first was an "unselfconscious" design with a young oak-hickory forest composition on the slope and floodplain forest species on the lower plain, just a few feet above the normal level of the Bronx River: blackgum, red maple, and a sycamore, with shrubs and wet-tolerant ferns, sedges, and forbs beneath the canopy. The second concept visibly displayed its "rivers and drifts." There were rivers of purple lovegrass and little bluestem, with flecks of the cobalt blue of spiderwort and orange of butterfly weed dotted among them in the sunny areas; various ferns, wild geranium, columbine, woodland phlox, and sedges in semishade to shade. The drifts cascading down the slope were composed of closely spaced gray birch and sassafras trees, and shrubs such as gray dogwood and dwarf bush honeysuckle. Blackgum and shrubs such as winterberry holly, spicebush, and buttonbush populated the plain in the lower area of the site. Of the two, I preferred this concept and so was pleased when the committee chose it. I had just eight months to develop a plan and oversee installation of more than ten thousand plants, including a row of flowering dogwood along the driveway at the top of the slope, which Gregory Long had requested to define the space more clearly. I wasn't wildly enthusiastic about the dogwoods in that location.

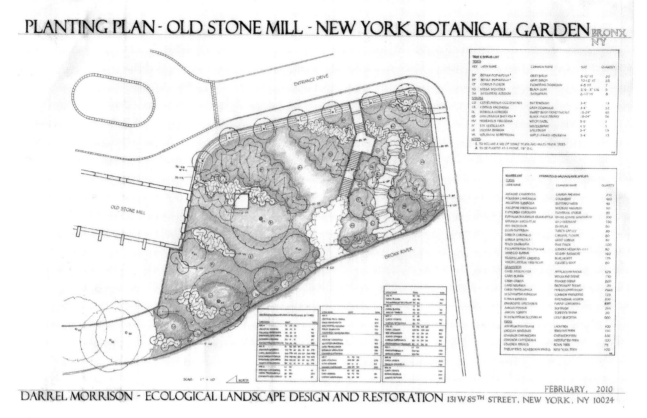

Old Stone Mill planting plan by Morrison, New York Botanical Garden, 2010.

In February I presented my clients with the final planting scheme, in a hand-drawn plan rendered in colored pencil which clearly depicted the rivers and drifts of vegetation. In addition to the dogwoods, the final plan included fifty-five closely spaced gray birches in two diagonal drifts down the slope which framed a view of the beautiful arched bridge over the river. Other woody species picked up the diagonal-drift theme: dwarf serviceberry near the top of the slope, gray dogwood at midslope, spicebush and winterberry holly just above the floodplain, and buttonbush along the riverbank, where it would be periodically inundated. Thirty-three species of herbaceous plants, in various combinations appropriate to the microhabitat, completed the picture in river-like forms reflecting and reinforcing the flow of the shrub drifts.

It was now only seven months until the dedication ceremony, and the NYBG staff sprang into action. Travis Beck, then gardens project manager, served as general overseer. Deanna Curtis sourced and ordered the required seventy-five trees and two hundred shrubs. Kristin Schleiter tracked down sources for the ten thousand herbaceous plants to be delivered in May and June. When the plants arrived, I worked with the staff on-site. At one-inch-equals-ten-feet scale, my drawing was too small to show placement of the individual plants, but zones indicated on the plan included the number of each species, and I placed the plants accordingly in the field.

That planting summer of 2010 turned out to be hot and humid. Temperatures in the 90s with high humidity made climbing the steep slope multiple times a day a challenge. Marc Wolf, one of my students in the NYBG courses, volunteered to be my field assistant, and together we staked locations for trees and shrubs and used color-coded flags for specific herbaceous plants. Then

Old Stone Mill from the bridge, NYBG, 2011. Photograph by Diana L. Drake.

a skilled crew from Dom's Landscaping of Darien, Connecticut, went to work.

During the planting process, Todd and Gregory dropped by to check on our progress. The birch drifts had gone in, but the row of seven dogwoods had not. I took the opportunity to point out the view from the top of the slope, with the river of little bluestem flowing down between the drifts of young birches leading to the arched bridge below. After I explained that this vista would be obstructed when we planted the dogwoods, Gregory agreed that they didn't need to be there. We found other good places to plant them.

Over the next five years while I was still living in New York City, I had multiple opportunities to watch the Old Stone Mill landscape change with the seasons. It was exciting to see the trees and shrubs growing and the herbaceous plants reproducing and "migrating" beyond their original locations. I like the idea that the landscape continues to evolve, but on a more recent visit, in fall 2018, I saw that the flowing river of space between the two drifts of birch trees was becoming obscured. Beneath my chosen early-suc-

View to the bridge with little bluestem and gray birches, NYBG. Photograph by Diana L. Drake.

Flowering dogwood, woodland phlox, and ragwort, Old Stone Mill, NYBG. Photograph by Julie Sakellariadis.

cessional tree species—the birches—there were not any later-successional species. (Where are you, squirrels, when I need you?) In the lower part of the site, volunteer trees—both native and non-native—were blocking the view of the bridge from the terrace. At the ground layer level, patches of invasive mugwort crowded out the Canada anemones and blue lobelias that had successfully colonized in the early years after their installation.

After discussing these observations with Todd and Jessica Schuler, ecologist and NYBG forest manager, we agreed that it was time for a reassessment. They had determined that the views to the mill and to the bridge were less important than they had been in the years immediately after the mill had been renovated, and I realized that the very legible (and, yes, beautiful) composition was ready to rise to the next level, one that would be less obviously designed. In late April 2019, Jessica and I met on the site with flags and stakes in hand to plan for that type of landscape. We would remove non-native trees and shrubs that had volunteered in the lower, semi-open area but permit native volunteers such as sweetgum to remain. Additional native trees of varying sizes—sycamore, blackgum, and musclewood—would be introduced in the low area. On the upper slope, we would "induce" succession by planting later-successional species at the edges of the birch drifts—white oak, northern red oak, shagbark hickory—and small shade-tolerant American beeches beneath the birches.

Todd came by as we were working. He remembered the more "natural" plan I had presented at our January 2010 meeting, and we realized that this new landscape would be a hybrid of the two alternatives. Knowing that the only thing constant in nature is change, we had no regrets about the scheme we had implemented in 2010 but accepted the idea that it could evolve in a new direction. After all, in twenty years, few visitors will suspect that the Old Stone Mill landscape was "designed." And that is okay.

Meanwhile, up the Hudson River, evolution was certainly occurring at Storm King Art Center too, where much of the land we originally planted in oats and alfalfa in the late 1990s was being converted to native grassland, bit by bit. I returned in 2010 to undertake an ambitious planting program in an extensive flat area to the west of Museum Hill. Once part of the gravel quarry for the New York Thruway, the area was essentially sand mixed with gravel. The three large islands to be planted totaled six acres. I specified a diverse seed mix for Bruce McCord to drill into them: little bluestem, big bluestem, Indiangrass, switchgrass, purpletop, and purple lovegrass, along with partridge pea. Immediately after the seeding, there was a two-month-long drought, meaning very few seeds germinated. Even the invasive spotted knapweed found it tough going in the parched soil.

View of tallgrasses (mounds planted 2008, flatland planting 2010–11) with Chakaia Booker's *Foci* (2010) and Mark di Suvero's *Neruda's Gate* (2005), Storm King Art Center. *Foci*, courtesy the artist. *Neruda's Gate*, lent by the artist and Spacetime C.C., New York. © Mark di Suvero, courtesy of the artist and Spacetime C.C. Photograph by Jerry L. Thompson. Courtesy Storm King Art Center.

Then, heavy rains came in August, and, lo and behold, we began to see single blades of native grasses valiantly emerging. I knew these would become increasingly larger clumps each year but recommended a supplemental overseeding the following May. In 2011, Mike Seaman, director of Facilities and Conservation, took over the native grass program, from seeding new areas to burning the increasingly large zones of tall grasses. The next spring, I hand-broadcast drifts of native forbs: butterfly weed, beebalm,

Canada wildrye in tallgrass planting, Storm King Art Center. Photograph by Jerry L. Thompson. Courtesy Storm King Art Center.

grass-leaved goldenrod, gray goldenrod, and smooth aster. The goal was to have increased species diversity in the form of impressionist-like dots of color within a tall grass matrix.

In 2011, while I was working at Storm King in the bucolic Hudson Valley, I began a project that took me downriver to the heart of Brooklyn, the Native Flora Garden Extension at the Brooklyn Botanic Garden. The original BBG Native Flora Garden had been designed and installed one hundred years earlier, in 1911, under the direction of Norman Taylor, the renowned botanist who was associated with both NYBG and BBG and author of *Botany: The Science of Plant Life*. That original design was based on a grid, with plants laid out according to taxonomy, that is, by family, genus, and species, rather than by plant community. As a result, the garden was not at all "naturalistic" in appearance.

The garden was redesigned in 1931 by Henry K. Svenson, chief botanist for the Vincent Astor Expedition to the Galapagos in 1930 and curator of BBG from 1930 to 1946. Svenson created an ecologically themed native garden, which was acknowledged to be the first in the United States. This 2.5-acre garden evolved over the next eighty years to become a mature forest, and sun-requiring plant communities such as eastern grasslands and pine barrens were shaded out. In 2011, an expansion of the native flora garden was proposed, one that was essentially open, in order to provide a place to display those sun-loving plant communities: savanna/woodland edge;

Pine barrens upland zone with butterfly weed, yellow-flowering baptisia, and little bluestem, Native Flora Garden Extension, Brooklyn Botanic Garden. Photograph by Diana L. Drake.

grasslands of Long Island's Hempstead Plains; and the pine barrens of Long Island and New Jersey. The pine barrens representation would include a spectrum of communities ranging from an upland sandy ridge to a pond and bog complex.

Scot Medbury, then-director of BBG, and garden staff proposed the extension and conducted a design charrette in early 2011 to come up with concepts. Mine was chosen, and I was asked to design the garden. The New York landscape architecture firm SiteWorks, led by Annette Wilkus, a University of Wisconsin alumna, was contracted to implement construction.

Once again, an important preparatory step for me was to work with a plant scientist. Uli Lorimer was then curator of the existing Native Flora Garden and had extensive knowledge of eastern grasslands and pine barrens. Uli and I made multiple field trips to the remnants of the tall grass prairies of the Hempstead Plains. There were many similarities between those eastern grasslands and the midwestern prairies I had worked with before, but there were also differences. These prairies were on the outwash of glacial sediment deposited on Long Island a hundred centuries ago. Before European settlement began, this was a landscape of ocean-like waves of big bluestem, little bluestem, Indiangrass, and switchgrass, with flecks of color provided by a sequence of forbs such as wild indigo, butterfly weed, blue-eyed grass, mountain mint, asters, and goldenrods.

Uli and I also made numerous trips to the New Jersey Pine Barrens, where I had first been while I was teaching at Rutgers. My fields trips with Uli gave me the opportunity to expand my knowledge of the plant species, distribution patterns, and aesthetics of this unique region. In some cases, we collected seed, with permission of the Pinelands Preservation Alliance. On one of our trips, Uli presented me with what has become one of my most cherished books, *The Vegetation of the New Jersey Pine-Barrens: An Ecologic Investigation* by John William Harshberger, published in 1916. A scientist who spent a quarter century carefully observing the ecology and botanical composition of the region, Harshberger was also sensitive to the aesthetics of the Pine Barrens. In the foreword to his book, he describes how "the shade of green used in the cloth cover corresponds with that of the evergreen foliage of the pitch-pines as illumined by the sun on a bright summer day." The book is deeply meaningful to me, for the vast amount of informa-

Boardwalk through the pond-bog complex in the pine barrens area, Native Flora Garden Extension, BBG. Wikimedia (CC BY-SA 4.0).

tion in it but also because it reminds me of those enjoyable trips with Uli and seeing the pitch-pines "illumined by the sun on a bright summer day."

I began my initial design for the garden by identifying zones for different plant community representations within the gently sloping acre of land extending southward from the original garden. The woodland edge / savanna, where the historic garden meets the new pine barrens and Hempstead Plains representations, formed a kind of boundary zone. The grassland communities of the Hempstead Plains crossed over three zones based on moisture: a xeric environment at the top of the slope, a dry-mesic zone at midslope, and then a mesic zone. I proposed two major zones in the pine barrens planting—the upland, with a dry, sandy ridge, and the lowland, with a pond and bog complex, as well as a symbolic white cedar–blackgum–red maple

Pitch pine, little bluestem, and sweet everlasting in the pine barrens upland zone, Native Flora Garden Extension, BBG. Photograph by Nancy Aten.

swamp, symbolic in that it has some of the key representatives of a pine barrens swamp but is only a tiny vignette as opposed to a true restoration of one.

After defining the plant community zones, I developed a circulation plan, in this case a system of sweeping curved pathways that allowed visitors to get close enough to see, touch, and smell the plants. A broad, gently curving boardwalk overlooks the pine barrens pond, and stabilized aggregate pathways lead to the pine barrens upland and the Hempstead Plains prairie continuum. SiteWorks developed specifications for the pathways and construction details for the built elements in the garden, including the boardwalk and an intimate twelve-foot-diameter limestone council ring, set in the middle of the Hempstead Plains grassland representation. Secondary mowed pathways in the upper part of the garden are planted with native grasses and the traffic-tolerant rush known as "path rush." The highly regarded soils consultant James Sotillo provided specifications for soil modifications matched with my plant community designations.

Having experienced the pine barrens in New Jersey and grasslands on Long Island, with Uli as my teacher, and immersing myself in the history of both regions, I was eager to begin placing plant species in the various community representations. As at the University of Wisconsin Arboretum, I selected plants based on three categories within each natural model: the characteristic *dominant* species, the most *abundant* species, and the *visual essence* species. The pine barrens uplands community included dominants such as the pitch pine and scrub oak; abundant species like sweetfern, bracken fern, little bluestem, Pennsylvania sedge, and bearberry; and prickly pear cactus for its distinctive form and color—the visual essence of the dry, sandy pine barrens environment. Rabbit tobacco, or sweet everlasting, also flourishes in open dry sand, and its distinctive silver-gray foliage and clusters of flowers added to the scene. In the placement of all the plants—trees, shrubs, and ground layer species—I tried to emulate the "directional drifts" seen in nature, sometimes very loosely aggregated, sometimes closely spaced, depending on the species.

SiteWorks supervised construction during planting in spring 2013, when I oversaw placement of plants, with Marc Wolf as my field assistant. The Greenbelt Native Plant Center, a New York City Department of Parks & Recreation nursery on Staten Island, propagated most of the plants, and the New York landscape services firm Steven Dubner Landscaping planted them as plugs, generally twelve to fifteen inches apart. In addition to the fifteen thousand plugs that were planted, Marc and I hand-broadcast sixteen pounds of native grass seed. Both the plants and the grasses were grown from seed collected by BBG and Greenbelt Nursery staff members on Long Island and in the New Jersey Pine Barrens.

The Native Flora Garden Extension grew dramatically throughout the summer of 2013. Not surprisingly, there were weeds, non-native opportunists that rush in wherever bare soil is available. As it happened, Uli was shorthanded that summer, with an acre of new planting to take care of, so I volunteered to cut and pull weeds on some occasions. On one warm afternoon of weeding in the upland pine barrens section, surrounded by little bluestem, rabbit tobacco, and beebalm, I felt movement and life all around me: small birds, butterflies, and bumblebees in flight, the little bluestem swaying in the breeze. And there was the curry-like smell of rabbit tobacco and pungent beebalm. Glancing a few feet to my left, I saw a prickly pear cactus we had planted. A young boy walking with his father saw it too.

Islands of native tallgrasses in the South Fields with Mark di Suvero's *Pyramidian* (1987/1998), *Beethoven's Quartet* (2003), *Mon Père, Mon Père* (1973–75), and *Mother Peace* (1969–70), Storm King Art Center. All works gift of the Ralph E. Ogden Foundation except *Beethoven's Quartet*, courtesy Tippet Rise Art Center. © Mark di Suvero, courtesy the artist and Spacetime C.C., New York. Photograph by Jerry L. Thompson. Courtesy Storm King Art Center.

"Look, Daddy, a cactus!" he cried. Nothing could have made me happier than hearing his excitement as he walked with his father into the pine barrens section of the Native Flora Garden—less than a hundred feet away from Flatbush Avenue in Brooklyn, New York.

While I was busy with the BBG designs, the meadows of Storm King had continued to mature, and by 2014 the six acres we originally planted in 2010 exemplified the potential of a diverse mix of native grasses with intermingling flowers, spurred on by controlled burning, to conquer the spotted knapweed. It still gives me a thrill to know that the mowed turf I saw on my first visit is now a meadow. On a windy day, you see the ocean-like waves that are so much a part of natural grasslands, whether on Long Island or in the Midwest. Storm King is indeed one big sculptural landscape into which a world-class collection of other sculptures has been placed. Always evolving, there will be changes in the landscape, but dramatic sweeps of tall grasses seem part of its identity.

8

RESTORING THE BEAUTY
OF THE WILD

The successful plantings at Storm King inspired me throughout the ongoing execution of a challenging residential garden project—a complete native landscape restoration for a historic house—the Round House, a modern architectural icon in Wilton, Connecticut. It is indeed circular and sits on a central pedestal near the high point of the site. I first saw it in 2014 while it was undergoing major restoration and redesign. On a day of pouring rain, my client and I, armed with umbrellas and ponchos, went out for a walk around the site, sometimes taking shelter and looking out over the amphitheatrical space from the terrace beneath the elevated house.

I soon learned that just as the Round House is no ordinary house, my client is no ordinary client. In *Siftings*, Jensen wrote that "clients are of all sorts. Those with a real understanding of landscaping are the very, very, few. Some know too much, or have an idea they do, and they are better left alone. Then there are those who want a garden because their neighbor has one, and I am afraid those are in the majority. But there are the few who have a real love for growing things."[1] This client is one of those few. She also has an eye for beauty—in art, in architecture, and in nature—and sees it not only in plants but in many other living things, from the chickens she cares for to the birds, butterflies, and bumblebees that now flit and fly through the six acres surrounding the home.

View from the Round House terrace, Wilton, CT. Photograph by Carol Betsch.

The Round House, designed by the architect Richard Foster, was featured in *Architectural Record* on its completion in 1968. Foster lived in the house with his family until his death in 2002. Ten years later, the current owners hired Mack Scogin Merrill Elam Architects of Atlanta to reconfigure the interior with the goal of maximizing views to the outdoors. After this remodel, which kept the exterior intact, the house was again featured in *Architectural Record*.[2]

My initial challenge was to replace the traditional lawn-dominated suburban landscape with native vegetation in community-like groupings. The sloping space is surrounded by a border of predominantly native mixed hardwood and conifer forest, which frames the open center. A small pond at the bottom of the slope is visible from the house. One of the first projects in the effort to "re-wild" the site was the replacement of more than an acre of turfgrass with an eastern meadow—the new panoramic view from the reconfigured interior of the house. On this slope I envisioned purple lovegrass, Canada wildrye, and little bluestem on the upper slope; then little bluestem, purple-top, and Indiangrass in the midsection; then a mix of Indiangrass, big blue-stem, and switchgrass in the lower, moister segment. I hand-broadcast drifts of quick-growing beebalm and black-eyed Susan, as well as an overlay of slower-to-establish forbs matched with the moisture level.

My client and I continue to meet each winter to plan a program for the next spring's planting, always with an eye toward increasing diversity, which leads to greater resilience—and, yes, more beauty in the landscape. An active participant in the planning and carrying out of the year's plan, she orders the plants and lines up a crew. In May, I place color-coded flags showing where drifts will go. My client, that unusual one who has a love of growing things, is there, planting alongside the crew.

Over the years, the two of us have collaborated on many other garden projects throughout the site. At the pond edge, we planted blue flag iris, cardinal flower, blue lobelia, swamp milkweed, cinnamon and sensitive ferns, rushes, and sedges. We developed a rock garden with boulders from the site placed into a slope and planted it with purple lovegrass, sundrops, blue-eyed grass, wild strawberry, butterfly weed, prairie phlox, woodland phlox, Pennsylvania sedge, and other species, located according to the varying need for sun and shade. Close to the house, on a rocky, dry slope with hot southwestern exposure, we planted purple lovegrass, little bluestem, butterfly weed, harebell, and even prickly pear cactus. For a moist woodland setting, we chose gray birch, dwarf bush honeysuckle, lady fern, Christmas fern, Pennsylvania sedge, Jacob's ladder, wild columbine, wild geranium, woodland phlox, and ragwort.

My client supports unconventional moves, like a switchgrass "hedge" that billows along each side of the narrow driveway and a grove of trembling aspen and staghorn sumac on a rocky bank just outside the house. The sumacs and aspens have grown to the height of the second story, where you can hear the aspen leaves tremble in the breeze and, in the fall, see the orange-to-scarlet leaves of sumac and yellow-to-golden leaves of the quaking aspens at eye level.

In 2016, my client and her husband acquired an additional two-acre plot to the east of the original Round House lot. A row of trees growing along the property line between the lots was removed. The space flows smoothly now, from the original lot to the adjacent one, which was already in a semi-wild state. An annual mowing program on that lot has revealed a traditional dry-laid stone wall, a reminder of an agricultural past. A zone of aging forest trees occupies the southern section of the site. From the edge of those woods, a new cluster of fifty young, early-successional trembling aspens emerges into the open field. Under the canopy of the old forest trees, twenty-five shade-tolerant American beech saplings have been planted. One day, they will become a part of the canopy, and their horizontal branches will retain their copper-turning-to-tan leaves through the winter.

Neither of us is enamored with cultivars of native species and we agree

Early-successional species: daisy fleabane, wild bergamot, and black-eyed Susan, Round House. Photograph by Jonathan D. Lippincott.

View to the Round House. Photograph by Jonathan D. Lippincott.

View to the chicken pen with ragwort, Pennsylvania sedge, and trembing aspen grove, **Round House.** Photograph by Rea David.

that we can't really improve on what was growing here long before we arrived. On one occasion, I recommended planting some elderberry shrubs in a moist area adjacent to the pond. When the nursery delivered a variegated cultivar, my client sent them back and found others of the species. On occasion, we have settled for cultivars of herbaceous species, but aberrations like orange-flowered purple coneflowers are not welcome in the Round House landscape. While there is some remaining lawn, there are no chemicals used in its management. Weeds in the various garden areas are not poisoned but are cut or pulled, and overseeding or infilling with additional plants provides competition for unwanted species.

At the end of our most recent planting day at the Round House, the two of us sat on the terrace under the house, overlooking the ever-changing landscape, cool drinks in hand. My client called out, "Ross . . . Ross!" Almost immediately, her pet rooster answered with friendly crowing from the chicken pen below. Surrounded by dozens of plants on the slope in front of us, alive with butterflies and bumblebees, we mused that the Round House, now more than a half century old, still seems futuristic, floating above the landscape like a flying saucer. And we agreed that the landscape is forward-looking in its way too. While it seeks to reintroduce native species and beauty from an earlier era, it is ahead of conventional twenty-first-century landscapes—those outdated designs that depend on chemicals, irrigation, and fossil fuels to keep them in a controlled, manicured, unchanging state. The Round House is a

View from the east lot, Round House. Photograph by Iwan Baan.

Wild bergamot along a path to the east lot meadow, Round House. Photograph by Jonathan D. Lippincott.

Sunlit opening at the edge of the woods, Round House. Photograph by Jonathan D. Lippincott.

living, evolving demonstration of the abundance of life, an ecosystem we can also emulate in a quarter of an acre or a rooftop planting area. There is sometimes a misperception that to adopt an ecological approach in designing our landscapes is somehow to deprive ourselves. But, to my client, who loves growing things, who loves life, there is a feast out there. The Round House landscape demonstrates that doing what is good for the earth and what is good for birds, butterflies, and bumblebees is good for us, too.

9

UNDER A MONTANA SKY

In the spring of 2006, I had the good fortune to begin consulting on landscape projects for a large ranch in Montana on the east side of the Rocky Mountains. The following spring, I began major planting projects in the building complex and vegetation restoration around some ponds that had earlier been dug on the site. Since then, I have continued to develop planting plans and vegetation management strategies for the ranch. The following musings on this singular landscape derived from a visit in late August 2017.

From my west-facing window of the ranch guesthouse is a view of gnarled limber pines. Some are dead, with rough-textured gray trunks and bare branches, and some are living, with clusters of short green needles. The reddish light that washed the Rockies to the west when I first awoke this morning has progressed through stages of orange, gold, and yellow. A warm tone remains on the grassy hillsides, which have not seen rain in nearly two months. There is movement everywhere. A magpie lands in the upper branches of a nearby tree and begins to pluck pine nuts out of a cone, and then moves on to another . . . and another. The pine branches bob and the clumps of narrow-bladed grasses beneath them sway in the wind. The thick, brittle leaves of an arrowleaf balsamroot rattle just outside my window. A perky striped chipmunk scurries across the rocky ground, leaps effortlessly onto the cut stump of an ancient limber pine, and suns himself on the warm, flat surface. A white butterfly flits by.

I step outside my room onto a raised stone terrace with two-inch-tall silver sage plants and flat mats of pussytoes growing in the spaces between the gray to brownish stone slabs. Over a decade has passed since I first designed these terraces. I walk down five broad stone steps on the west side, past the clump of crisp, rattling balsamroot leaves and the perky chipmunk's sunny pine stump.

A two-foot-wide, dry-laid stone path winds through the clusters of dwarf gnarly pines to the west. I remember how much fun it was to lay out that path,

View of the native landscape from the guesthouse terrace, Montana ranch. Photograph by Carol Betsch.

Limber pines, balsamroot, and native grasses near the guesthouse, Montana ranch. Photograph by Carol Betsch.

placing colored flags through the clumps of pines, alternately in the open, then enclosed in a small pine grove, and then out into the open again. Sunlight and shadow, prospect and refuge. The curves in the narrow path are not broad, river-like curves but those of a winding stream. There is a bit of mystery where low-branched pines partially block the view and then open up to reveal blue-gray mountain peaks on the distant horizon. Next, a rustic circular wall is revealed, a council ring, twelve feet in diameter with a three-foot-wide entrance portal. Across from this opening, a preexisting stone slab encrusted in silver and orange lichens interrupts the constructed stone circle, thrusting upward at a 45-degree angle. Inside the ring, other lichen-covered slabs are loosely distributed, with tiny fine-textured grasses, dwarf blazingstars, and other diminutive plants growing between them. Similar species are sparsely sprinkled in the gravelly soil outside the ring, and flat, horizontal junipers, surprisingly green, provide colorful accents throughout.

During my first exploratory walks into this area—pre-path and pre–council ring—I felt humbled by the composition of beautiful tiny plants in this harsh, dry environment. I remember thinking that I had never designed anything this beautiful. When it came time to do remedial, healing planting along the new pathway and seating area, I made every effort to use species that were already present. Now I'm pleased that it is impossible to see my design or

Council ring, Montana ranch. Photograph by Darrel Morrison.

Balsamroot on the slope near the guesthouse, Montana ranch. Photograph by Carol Betsch.

to differentiate between the plants we introduced as plugs and those that were already here. Invisible design.

I walk the winding path back to the guesthouse. After a stop for water, I head out on a second broad pathway that curves to the southeast on a downhill slope. The limber pines here are larger and more widely spaced, making this a path of a very different character. Instead of winding between little groves, this path is a wide arc ending under a solitary ancient limber pine. Beneath its canopy, gnarled roots have been clasping an angular lichen-covered stone outcrop for at least two centuries of hot, drying summers, bitter winds, snow, and ice of subzero winters, and the hundred-mile-an-hour "chinook" winds of spring.

I reach the picturesque old pine. There are four blocks of stone here, approximately two-foot cubes set in an informal arrangement with twisted pine branches arching over them. This is a place of panoramic views and vast spaces. As I sit on one of the cubes, looking southeast, I see a high, nearly flat plateau on the horizon and, to the south and southwest, Deep Creek winding through a valley below. Beyond the creek, layers of mountains rise majesti-

Morrison sitting under the ancient limber pine, Montana ranch. Photograph by Carol Betsch.

Bison grazing in the valley, Montana ranch. Photograph by Carol Betsch.

cally from the valley. The awe-inspiring grandeur of these mountains contrasts with the intricate, close-up landscape of fine-textured tan and golden grasses and diminutive wildflowers. I walk the arc of the pathway back up the slope toward the guesthouse. The plantings we did here in 2007, like those along the council ring path, are almost all of species that were here long before we arrived. And again, I can't differentiate between the two.

I walk up to the terraces on the south side of the guesthouse, paved with dry-laid stones fitting together like puzzle pieces interlocked by beds of low-growing plants. During the original design phase, I produced a series of "dot" drawings at a scale of one-quarter inch to one foot with quarter-inch

Limber pines, balsamroot, and native grasses, Montana ranch. Photograph by Carol Betsch.

color-coded dots representing different species of grasses and forbs. The dot drawings helped me create plant distribution patterns that (in my mind) emulated the rivers and drifts I had seen in the naturally evolving landscape. I typically started with a framework of grass species, a matrix within which the forbs were placed as individuals or their own "sub-drifts."

I walk on generous porches to the north side of the guesthouse, where a kitchen/office building and an open parking structure define the entrance court. In the center of the gravel court is a stone-curbed circle filled with Idaho fescue, blue grama grass, various forb species, and a sun-bleached limber pine trunk lying off-center in the circle. A harebell's remaining blue-violet bell-like flowers bob in the breeze. I look back at the front entrance walk. Unlike the winding pathway to the council ring, this walk is eight feet wide, straight, and composed of sharp-cut rectangular stones, making it clear that this is the main entrance.

Another path runs from the guesthouse complex to the main house. If the council ring path is a winding stream, this path, six feet wide and thirteen hundred feet long, is a river. It hugs the slope in a gentle downward arc, a decision requiring minor grading on both the upper and lower sides of the walkway. We planted low-growing plants—lupines, penstemons, pussytoes, and short grasses—into the disturbed zone. In the end, this revegetation project was a real collaboration: we planted some "parent" plants and let nature do the rest. It's hard to tell who did what, and that is not important.

Being involved in the planning, design, and management of a specific land-

Native vegetation restoration at a constructed pond, Montana ranch. Photograph by Carol Betsch.

Path to the council ring, Montana ranch. Photograph by Carol Betsch.

scape for a decade offers the landscape designer a rare luxury—the opportunity to see fledgling plants establishing, flowering, and even migrating within a dynamic, shifting composition. This experience is often accompanied by the challenge of working in disturbed environments, such as the construction sites of the guesthouse complex and the main house. Planting each species represented by a colored dot in the pretty drawings is only the beginning—the stage setting for an ongoing drama. From the outset, some plants struggle, while others thrive; some politely "stay put," while others increase, seemingly exponentially. This ongoing ebb and flow is affected by the vagaries of any one year's temperature and precipitation patterns, the presence or absence of certain soil micro-organisms, and the troublesome characters who walk onto the stage—the smooth brome, crested wheatgrass, cheatgrass, and others not in the script.

The ranch owners and ranch manager fully appreciate the challenges and the complexity of "re-wilding" disturbed landscapes and are responding with a range of practices. These include overseeding problem planting areas with desirable native species, experimenting with cutting and mowing strategies, and introducing native plants known to be allelopathic, capable of exuding chemicals that suppress unwanted competitors. A bison herd is permitted to graze periodically in the building complex area.

It's almost sunset time. I walk the winding pathway through the limber pines to the council ring. The pines' shadows are lengthening as I sit on the rustic circular wall. A chipmunk pokes through a tiny opening between the rocks and pauses to look quizzically at me. ("What is *he* doing in *my* council ring?") As I look westward, the sun is just above the horizon. The diminutive grasses, backlit with golden light, are luminous. They continue to bob in the light evening breeze. The air is taking on a chill, a hint of fall. As the sun sets, a sense of well-being settles over me. I feel infinite gratitude for the privilege of working with clients who love this place and have made provisions for its protection and preservation, ensuring that the beauty of the wild will live on here in perpetuity.

EPILOGUE:
BACK TO THE PRAIRIE

As much as I loved being in New York, designing landscapes based on natural models, seeing masterpieces in the museums, hearing great music in the concert halls, and enjoying the companionship of neighbors down the hall, the time came for me to go home again. I felt the urge to be back in the Midwest, where my own roots mingled with those of big bluestem and purple prairie clover, and where I felt the tug of now three younger generations of my family. I continue to make fairly frequent work-related trips to New York, where I keep up with the landscape projects at Storm King, NYBG, BBG, and the Round House and still see my "New York family" on West 85th Street.

In Madison, I am never far from some of my all-time favorite natural landscapes, ones I came to love in the 1970s, and I have brought a miniaturized version of a dry prairie into a series of cedar planting boxes that line the west side of my second-floor terrace, right outside my apartment living room. So I am never far from little bluestem, purple prairie clover, mountain mint, and another thirty species of native prairie plants. I see the backlit gray-green leaves of little bluestem on hot summer afternoons, and the backlit coppery leaves of those same grasses through the winter. Throughout the year, they sway gracefully, reminding me of many happy days I have spent in protected or restored prairies and other natural landscapes in many places.

As an honorary senior faculty associate in the Department of Planning

Prairie Indian-plantain, a threatened species, Morrison Prairie & Forest Preserve, Driftless Area, WI. Photograph by Jennifer Filipiak.

Morrison with David Clutter, former executive director, Driftless Area Land Conservancy, Morrison Prairie & Forest Preserve, 2018. Photograph courtesy DALC.

and Landscape Architecture, I give occasional lectures, participate in design critiques, lead field trips with Friends of the University Arboretum, and co-lead tours of the Native Plant Garden with its curator, Susan Carpenter. Life in Madison is rich with former students and faculty colleagues from thirty, forty, or fifty years ago, as well as newer faculty members.

The twenty acres of high-quality prairie and forest in Iowa County, where I once thought I would live, is now officially the Morrison Prairie & Forest Preserve, owned and managed by the Driftless Area Land Conservancy. Although there will never be a cabin there, I can still visit and see the bird's-foot violets and puccoons, along with scores of other species that have lived there for centuries and, thanks to the conservancy, will continue to thrive into the future.

NOTES

CHAPTER 2

1. Olmsted Brothers to A. B. Storms, President of Iowa State College, June 2, 1906; Iowa State University Library Digital Collections.
2. Robert William Werle, "A Historical Review and Analysis of the Iowa State University Landscape from 1858 to 1966," master's thesis, 1966.
3. The city planner Eldridge Lovelace (1913–2008), a student of Harland Bartholomew at the University of Illinois, spent his entire forty-six-year career employed by his mentor.
4. Harland Bartholomew (1889–1989), one of the most prolific and accomplished urban planners of his generation, contributed to more than 6,000 projects during a career lasting more than five decades. In 1959, he reorganized his firm as Harland Bartholomew & Associates, City Planners, Civil Engineers, and Landscape Architects.
5. Claire Avis, a graduate of Washington University in St. Louis, was the chief planner in the Honolulu office of Harland Bartholomew & Associates until 1956, when she was transferred to the main office in St. Louis. "Hawaii Chapter," *Landscape Architecture Magazine* 46 (January 1956): 102.
6. Robert Cole Simonds, a city planner, was the son of Robert Ossian Simonds and the grandson of the landscape architect Ossian Cole Simonds.

CHAPTER 3

1. Joseph Paul Kondis (1931–2015) would go on to become chief of the engineering and design division for the commission.
2. John R. Bracken (1891–1979), author of *Planting Design* (1953), was the head of the Penn State landscape architecture department from 1926 to 1957 and after his retirement joined the faculty of the University of Wisconsin.
3. Edith Roberts (1886–1946) studied under the ecologist Henry Chandler Cowles at the

University of Chicago before becoming a professor at Vassar, where she founded the Dutchess County Ecological Laboratory to promote the study of native plants. Elsa Rehmann was an established landscape architect, writer, and teacher when the two collaborated on *American Plants for American Gardens*. Their book is considered the first US publication promoting ecological principles as the foundation for an approach to landscape design.

4. Edith A. Roberts and Elsa Rehmann, *American Plants for American Gardens* (New York: Macmillan, 1929), 35.

5. Lucy Lawliss, Caroline Loughlin, and Lauren Meier, eds., *The Master List of Design Projects of the Olmsted Firm, 1857–1979* (National Association for Olmsted Parks et al., 2008), lists "Rock Creek Park, Washington, D.C.," with plans drawn 1907–1945.

6. A graduate of the University of Illinois, Thurman Donovan (1924–1984) launched his practice in Gaithersburg, MD, in the late 1950s and later expanded his firm as Donovan, Feola, Balderson & Associates.

7. Eric Sundback established a Christmas tree farm in West Virginia and became famous, with his horticulturalist wife Gloria, for supplying the annual White House Christmas tree, most recently after winning the national Christmas tree contest in 2009.

CHAPTER 4

1. Aldo Leopold (1887–1948), one of the foremost ecologists and conservationists of his generation, inspired wilderness advocacy through his bestselling book, *A Sand County Almanac, And Sketches Here and There* (1949; reprint Oxford University Press, 1989).

2. Leopold, *A Sand County Almanac*, 96.

3. John T. Curtis (1913–1961), botanist and ecologist, wrote *The Vegetation of Wisconsin: An Ordination of Plant Communities* (Madison: University of Wisconsin, 1959), among several other catalogs of native plants.

4. P. M. Bardi, *The Tropical Gardens of Burle Marx* (New York: Reinhold, 1964). Pietro Maria Bardi, a professor and art dealer, was a cofounder of the São Paulo Museum of Art.

5. A. E. Bye Jr., "What You See: Landscape Luminosity," *Landscape Architecture Magazine* 56 (April 1966): 207–8.

6. The landscape architect Jens Jensen (1860–1951) emigrated from Denmark and became the foremost advocate of the native midwestern landscape, working to preserve the prairie and educating future stewards of the land at his school, The Clearing.

7. Henry Chandler Cowles's writings include "The Ecological Relation of the Vegetation on the Sand Dunes of Lake Michigan," *Botanical Gazette* 27 (February 1899): 95–117.

8. Jens Jensen, *Siftings* (1939; Baltimore: Johns Hopkins University Press, 1990), 38.

9. Ibid., 47

10. Ibid., 66.

11. Floyd Allen Swink's *Plants of the Chicago Region* (1969) was reprinted four times, most recently in 1994.

12. Jensen, *Siftings*, 1.

13. Ibid., 6.

14. Jens Jensen founded Friends of Our Native Landscape, a community group advocating wilderness stewardship, in 1913.

15. Darrel G. Morrison, "Restoring the Midwestern Landscape," *Landscape Architecture Magazine* 65 (October 1975): 398–403.
16. Darrel G. Morrison, "Research: Vegetation and Iron Ore Tailings," *Landscape Architecture Magazine* 71 (July 1981): 480–81.
17. Tom Hunt served as a consultant to the Jackson County Iron Company through 1983, the year he received his MSLA degree, and then went on to pursue his PhD at UW Madison.

CHAPTER 5

1. It was later included in the NPS publication *Currents* (2017), under the title "Sustainable Military Earthworks Management," edited by Shaun Eyring, manager of the NPS Resource Planning and Compliance Program, Northeast Region, and Lucy Lawliss, lead, Park Cultural Landscape Program, National Center for Cultural Resources, NPS; available online at https://www.nps.gov/tps/how-to-preserve/currents/earthworks/index.htm.
2. Nancy M. Aten is principal of Landscapes of Place, a landscape architecture and ecological restoration firm based in Mequon, WI.

CHAPTER 6

1. The *Plant Field Guide* is available online at https://www.nyu.edu/content/dam/nyu/facilitiesContMgt/documents/gardenshop/plant-field-guide.pdf.

CHAPTER 8

1. Jens Jensen, *Siftings* (1939; Baltimore: Johns Hopkins University Press, 1990), 71.
2. Anna Fixsen, "Restoring Richard T. Foster's Round House," *Architectural Record*, June 1, 2017.

ACKNOWLEDGMENTS

First of all, my thanks to Robin Karson, founder and executive director of the Library of American Landscape History, for encouraging me to write this book and for her sage advice at the very beginning: "Just tell stories!" she said. So that is what I did.

Next, many thanks to her colleagues at LALH, Sarah Allaback and Carol Betsch, whose insightful editing made it a more concise—and better—book. Thanks to Carol, too, for tracking down illustrations and for digitizing my own decades-old slides. And last but far from least, I thank Jonathan Lippincott, associate director of LALH, for making *Beauty of the Wild* a work of art itself through his exquisite design.

I also want to thank Signe Holtz, my former University of Wisconsin–Madison graduate student, who converted my handwritten manuscript into digital form and sent it off to LALH, always enthusiastically and on time.

My thanks as well to the many photographers whose work graces these pages. In addition to Carol Betsch, I want especially to acknowledge Robert Jaeger, whose photographs at the University of Wisconsin–Madison Arboretum capture the spirit of the place so vividly; Susan Carpenter, whose superb photographs of the Native Plant Garden trace its development since she became curator in 2003 and whose "plant portraits" are interspersed throughout; Jerry L. Thompson, who has beautifully photographed two decades of evolution and change in our native tallgrass plantings at Storm King Art Center; Diana L. Drake, for her evocative images of the Old Stone Mill landscape at the New York Botanical Garden and the Native Flora Garden Extension at Brooklyn Botanic Garden; Nancy Aten, for capturing the winter beauty of native flora at BBG; Julie Sakellariadis, for her quintessential image of the woods phlox at the Old Stone Mill; Jennifer Filipiak, executive director of the Driftless Area Land Conservancy, who went above and beyond to photograph a prairie/forest preserve in Iowa County, Wisconsin, a place that is close to my heart; and Rea David, for her wonderful photographs of the wild gardens at the Round House.

To my colleagues at the University of Wisconsin, who helped me in developing a philosophy of landscape design and restoration, I owe special thanks, particularly William Tishler, Evelyn Howell, and John Harrington. I want to express my appreciation also to my former colleagues at the University of Georgia College of Environment and Design, several of whom have become lifelong friends.

And a very large collective thanks to the hundreds of students I have had the pleasure of teaching—and learning from—during the past half century. As teaching and research assistants as well, they provided me invaluable new insights and inspiration.

It is my very good fortune to have such a loving family. My sons, Jon and Scott, and their families have always been there for me, including during the months I have been absorbed in writing this book: Scott and Nomita Morrison; Jon and Margaret Morrison and their children, Basil, Madeline, and Mari, Mari's husband Andrew Martin, and their children, Mirabella and Luca.

Finally, I thank Gary Gill, whose steady and steadying support and companionship I have enjoyed since the day we first met for a cup of coffee on December 31, 2018. He was 79; I was 81. That conversation over coffee lasted four hours. Now we begin many of our days with a morning hike in the prairie and end them on my terrace watching little bluestem in cedar planting boxes waving in the breeze, backlit by the setting sun. The conversation continues as we sip our wine and talk about how these will be the times we will look back on and remember . . . when we get old.

Since 1992, LALH books, exhibitions, and films have been funded by individuals who care deeply about landscape, history, and American culture. By educating the public, LALH encourages preservation of beloved landscapes and inspires new designs that connect people with nature.

Beauty of the Wild was made possible with the generous support of the following:

Anonymous

Rea David and Judd Tully
Furthermore: a program of the J. M.
    Kaplan Fund
Janine Luke

Cynthia Hewitt and Dan Holloway
William and Joyce O'Neil
    Charitable Trust

Lauren Belfer and Michael Marissen
    Fund
Lynn Bjorkman and Arnold Alanen,
    Hon. ASLA
Nancy Frederick
Michael and Evelyn Jefcoat
Keith N. Morgan, FSAH
Mark K. Morrison, FASLA
Barbara Robinson
Barbara Slifka

Adele Ashkar
Craig and Diana Barrow
Susan and Robert Grese, ASLA
Gary Hilderbrand, FASLA
David Kamp, FASLA

Francis R. Kowsky
Darwina Neal, FASLA
Elizabeth and Ted Rogers
Nicole Ward
Lauren Wheeler
David W. White

Ann Abadie
Debra Adamsons
Nancy Aten, ASLA
Josephine Bush
David Carlson, ASLA
Susan Carpenter
Ann Cicarella
David B. Coleman
George W. Curry, FASLA
Ralph D'Amato Jr., ASLA
James C. Differding, ASLA
Jeffrey J. Dyer
Royce Earnest
Nancy Fee
Ian Firth, FASLA
Elisabeth French
Paul Ganshert
Todd Haiman
Nancy Lyons Hannick, ASLA
Jean Marie Hartman

Marian Hill
Thomas Hunt and Nancy Nye
Kris Jarantoski
Barry W. Jeffries, ASLA
Katherine Koch
Lucy Lawliss, ASLA
Jane MacLeish
Mr. and Mrs. Joseph H. McGee
Friedrike Merck
Kathleen M. Metz
John Franklin Miller
David Mladenoff
Mary E. Myers
Deborah Nevins
Karen Oberhauser
Anne Petri
Roy and Laurie Regozin
Margaret E. Richardson
Mark Robison and Melissa Bannon
Michael Schneider
Karen Sebastian, ASLA
Natalie Shivers, AIA
Judith Z. Stark
Frederick Steiner

Robert A. M. Stern, FAIA
Margaret D. Sullivan
Bill Thomas, Chanticleer
    Foundation
William Tishler, FASLA
Caitlin and Mark Traver
Melissa Tufts
Judith H. Whitney-Terry
Marc Wolf and Craig Thompson
Louise Wrinkle

Steven Bopp
Richard Childs and John Funt
Bruce Ferguson
Lawrence Hott and Diane Garey
Gregory Levine
William and Judith Locke
Romalda Lopat
Judith K. Major
Hugh C. Miller, FAIA
Magda Salvensen
Barbara Shear
Craig Smith
Sally and Mark Zelonis, Hon. ASLA

INDEX

Page numbers in italics refer to illustrations.

Abraham's Woods (University of Wisconsin), 107
Acadia National Park (ME), *33*
Alanen, Arnold, 66
allelopathic plants, 163
American Plants for American Gardens (Roberts and Rehmann), 32–33, *34,* 35–36, 70, 118, 169–70n3; reprint with Morrison foreword (1996), 101
American Society of Landscape Architects (ASLA), 1959 annual meeting, 25
Anderson, J. Robert (landscape architect), 87
Apostle Islands National Lakeshore (WI), 36–37
Appleton, Jay, *The Experience of Landscape,* 84
Arch, The (Calder), 97, 102
Archer, Rick (architect), 87
Armstrong, Gregory, 102
Arnold Arboretum, Harvard University, 24
Aten, Nancy, 117, 171n2
Atlanta History Center project, 89–92, *90, 91,* 94
Avis, Claire (landscape architect), 25, 169n5

Avoca Prairie (WI), *46*
Babize, Mollie, 94
balds. *See* grassy balds
Bardi, Pietro Maria, 170n4; *The Tropical Gardens of Burle Marx,* 42–43, 85
Barreto, Henrique Lahmeyer de Mello (ecologist), 43
Bartenieff, George, 122
Bartholomew, Harland, 169n4
Battery Park City (New York City), 117
Bayfield, WI, design and planning guidelines for, 36–37
Beauty of the Wild (Goodman), 56
Beck, Travis, 128–29
Beethoven's Quartet (di Suvero), *99, 140*
Big Woods (Greenwood Plantation, GA), *75,* 75–77
Black Balsam Knob (NC), *70, 71,* 71–72
Black Rock Forest (NY), 122–23, *122, 123*
bogs, *45;* in Brooklyn Botanic Garden, Native Flora Garden Extension project, 136–37, *137;* Hawley Bog Preserve (MA), 94
Booker, Chakaia, *Foci, 133*
Botany: The Science of Plant Life (Taylor), 135
Bracken, John R., 32, 34, 43, 169n2; ecological approach, 101
Bradley, Nina Leopold, 65
Brooklyn Botanic Garden, Native Flora Garden Extension project, 134–41,

135, 137, 138; circulation plan, *137,* 138–39; council ring, 139; "drifts," 139; original garden design (1911) and redesign (1931), 134–35; pine barrens representations, upland, lowland, and swamp, *135,* 136, *137, 138;* plants used, *135, 138,* 139–40; pond-bog complex, *137;* purpose, 135–36; zones, 136–38
Bruner, Cathie, 61
Burle Marx, Roberto, 42–43, 59–60, 85, 93–94, 115; César da Silva and, 109–10; Georgia Institute of Technology lecture, 85; Sítio (home and garden; Guaratiba, Brazil), 85, 109
butterflies and other pollinators, 55
burns. *See* controlled burns
Bye, A. E., 43, 59, 84, 101; "Landscape Luminosity," 43–44
Byrne, Ken, 94

Calder, Alexander, *The Arch,* 97, 102
Carpenter, Susan, 109, 167
Carter, Arthur (sculptor), 125
Carter, Jimmy, 79
CELA (Council of Educators in Landscape Architecture), annual meeting (1981), 65; and founding of *Landscape Journal,* 65–66
Chesser Prairie, Okefenokee Swamp, 78, 79
Christy, Stephen, 59–59

Clark, Robert M., *Native Woodland Garden in Schwartz Plaza: Plant Field Guide,* 126

Clay, Grady, 61

Clearing, The (Ellison Bay, WI), 48–59; Nancy Aten at, 117; Cliff House, 57–58; Council Ring, 56, 57; Lodge, *48,* 48, 56, 58; Morrison visit to (1970), 50; music at, 56; native vegetation course, 51–52, 54; setting and buildings, 50, *51, 52, 53,* 52–53, 58; trails, *53,* 53–54, 57–58; George Ziegler and, 48–49. *See also* Jensen, Jens

Clemons, Rodney, 90, 92

Cloisters, the (New York City), 25, 117

Clutter, David, *167*

Collens, David, 97

Columbia University, Master of Landscape Design program, 122

controlled burns: benefits of, 64; at GE prairie project, *62,* 63–64; by Native Americans, 9, 63, 114–15; at Storm King, 114–15, 133, 141

Conway School of Landscape Design (MA), 93–94

Corson, Ada, 50

Council of Educators in Landscape Architecture. *See* CELA

council rings: at Brooklyn Botanic Garden, Native Flora Garden Extension, 139; at The Clearing, 56, 57; Jensen on, 50; at Montana ranch project, 155–56, *156,* 163

cover crops, 61, 99–102

Cowles, Henry Chandler, 49, 169–70n3, 170n7

Cudnohufsky, Walter, 93

Cumberland Island (GA), 76

CUNA Mutual Insurance Company headquarters project (Madison, WI), 60–61, 93–94

Curtis, Deanna, 129

Curtis, John T., 170n3; *The Vegetation of Wisconsin,* 41–42, 102

Curtis Prairie, University of Wisconsin Arboretum, 39–41, *40, 102, 105, 106*

curves: Jensen on, 49; in path and walkway design, 47, 105, 138, 155

D'Amato, Ralph (landscape architect), 36

da Silva, César, 109–10

Danadjieva, Angela (landscape architect), 93

Deere, John, 10

design philosophy and concepts: aesthetic essence; 85; art, influence of, 18, 89, 94, 134; Bracken, influence of, 101; Burle Marx, influence of, 42–43, 115; "design by subtraction," 56; diversity in planting, value of 76–77, 85, 134, 141, 145; "dot" drawings (planting plans), 159–60, 163; dominant, abundant, and visual essence species, 139; drawing process and, 22–23, 83–84, 88, *88,* 104; "drifting" plants, 35, 126, 129, 139, 145 (*see also* "rivers and drifts" concept); ecological approach, 33, 36, 66, 89, 94, 101, 151; Jensen, influence of, 48–50, 59–60; luminosity, 43–44, 136–37, 163; mass:space concept and plans: 35–36, 60, 103–5, *104,* 117; music, in design process, 83–84, 93, 104–5; "mystery–complexity–coherence–legibility" concept, 85; native cultivars, 146–48; and native plant communities, 32–33, 35, 42; "prospect-refuge" theory, 84; "rivers and drifts" concept, 99, 127–28, 130, 160; Roberts and Rehmann's *American Plants for American Gardens,* influence of, 32–33, 70, 101, 118; and scientific research, 85; "visual essence," 47, 55, 88–89, 92, 102, 139

Des Moines Art Center, 18

District of Columbia Department of Highways and Traffic, Morrison at, 36

di Suvero, Mark: *Beethoven's Quartet, 99, 140; Mon Père, Mon Père, 140; Mother Peace, 140; Neruda's Gate, 133; Pyramidian, 99, 140*

diversity in planting, value of, 76–77, 85, 134, 141, 145

Dom's Landscaping (Darien, CT), 130

Donovan, Thurman (landscape architect), 35, 170n6

Doty, Carol, 59

drawing and painting: in design work, 22–23, 83–84, 88, *88,* 104; in field studies, 46, 92; and "visual essence," 47, 55

"drifts": in planting design, 35, 126, 129, 139, 145; natural, 85, 139; "sub-drifts," 160; and topography, 125. *See also* "rivers and drifts" concept

Driftless Area (WI): 110–11, *114;* Morrison property in (now Morrison Prairie & Forest Preserve), 113–15, 119, 167

Driftless Area Land Conservancy, 167

Dubitsky, Matt, 125–26

Duke, George, "Love" movement from *Muir Woods Suite,* 83, 104–5

Dutchess County Ecological Laboratory, 169–70n3

early-successional species. *See* successional species

Eaton, Leonard, *Landscape Artist in America: The Life and Work of Jens Jensen,* 49–50

ecological approach to landscape design, 33, 66, 89, 94, 101, 112, 151; *American Plants for American Gardens* (Roberts and Rehmann) and, 32–33, 36; John R. Bracken and, 32, 101; Henry K. Svenson and, 135

ecology, science of, 39–41; Henry Cowles and, 49; John T. Curtis and, 41–42; Dutchess County Ecological Laboratory, 169–70n3; John William Harshberger and, 136–37; Eugene Odum and, 84–85; and vegetation sampling, 45–47

Edgar, Alvin, 22

Effigy Mounds National Monument (IA), *13*

Endless Column (Streeter), 98, 102

environmental psychology, 85

ephemeral pools, 73, *73,* 89, 92, 107

exotic species, 115

Experience of Landscape, The (Appleton), 84

Experience of Nature, The (Kaplan and Kaplan), 85, 93

Fair Lane (Henry Ford estate, Dearborn, MI), 49, 93

Firth, Ian (landscape architect), 67, 86–86

Fitzsimmons, John R., 19

Fleming, Laurence, *Roberto Burle Marx: um retrato* (Roberto Burle Marx: A Portrait), 110

Foci (Booker), *133*

Ford, Henry, Fair Lane estate (Dearborn, MI), 49, 93

Forrest, Todd, 126–27, 130, 132

forests: Black Rock Forest (NY), 122–23, *123;* at The Clearing, 52–53; in Driftless Area property, 113, 167; in Georgia Piedmont, 89; longleaf pine (*see* longleaf pine savannas); New York Botanical Garden, Old Stone Mill representations, 127–28, 132; redwood, 104; at Round House, 144, 146; in saltmarsh areas, 77–78; sampling of, 47; at Toft Point, 54; at Storm King Art Center, 100; University of Wisconsin Arboretum, Native Plant Garden representations, *41*, 105, 107

Fort Belvoir (Fairfax County, VA), military service at, 28–29

Fort Hood (TX), military training at, 26–28

Fort Tryon Park (New York City), 117

Foster, Richard (architect), 144

Fredericksburg & Spotsylvania National Military Park (VA), consulting project, 94

Free Ride Home (Snelson), 98

Friends of Our Native Landscape, 58, 170n14

Friends of the Arboretum (University of Wisconsin), 103

Fulkerson, Mertha, 49–51, 58

Gantry Plaza State Park (Queens, NY), 117

Garden Club of Georgia, 67

Geiger, Jodi, and Walden Park project, 59–60

General Electric Medical Systems Division project (Pewaukee, WI), *61, 62,* 61–63

Georgia Piedmont region: granite outcrops, *72,* 72–73; native plant communities, 70–72, 89

Gimmler, Elizabeth (landscape architect), 50

Glass, Philip, "Low" Symphony, 83

Glenwood Children's Park (Madison, WI), 49

Goldsworthy, Andy, *Storm King Wall, 100*

Goodman, Kenneth Sawyer, *Beauty of the Wild* (masque), 56

Grand Prairie, Okefenokee Swamp, 79

granite outcrops, 89–92, *90, 91;* native plant communities, *72,* 72–73

grasslands, eastern U.S., 86, 97, 136–37; and Brooklyn Botanic Garden, Native Flora Garden Extension project, 136–39; moisture zones of Hempstead Plains (Long Island), 137; native plant species, 136; similarity to tallgrass prairies, 97, 136. *See also* Storm King Art Center project

grassy balds, *70, 71,* 71–72

Greenbelt Native Plant Center (NYC Department of Parks & Recreation), 139

Greene Prairie, University of Wisconsin Arboretum, *40*

Greentree Foundation, 75

Greenwood Plantation (GA), *75,* 75–77

Grese, Robert, 93

Grieg, Edvard, "Wedding Day at Troldhaugen," 56

Grosvenor, Robert (sculptor), 97

groundcovers, 24; native plants as, 70

"The Growth of an Artist: Jens Jensen and Landscape Architecture" (Christy), 58–59

Guide to Sustainable Earthworks Management (NPS), 94, 171n1

Gullatte, Gary (landscape architect), 89

Hanson, A. Maurice, 19, 21

Hardell, Julie, 64

Hare & Hare (Kansas City, MO), 18

Harland Bartholomew & Associates (St. Louis), 169n4; Morrison at 24–26

Harper, Samuel, 60

Harshberger, John William, *The Vegetation of the New Jersey Pine-Barrens,* 136–37

Hartman, Jean Marie, 118

Harvard University, Arnold Arboretum, 24

Hatch Act (1887), 64

Hauptman, Dawna. *See* Morrison, Dawna Hauptman

Hawley Bog Preserve (Hawley, MA), 94

Heery, George T. (architect), 89

Heggie's Rock (granite outcrop, Appling, GA), *72, 73,* 72–73, 89

Hempstead Plains (Long Island), 97; and Brooklyn Botanic Garden, Native Flora Garden Extension project, 136–39

Hengst, Gretel, 64

High Ledges Wildlife Sanctuary (Shelburne, MA), 94

Holtz, Signe, and *Landscape Journal,* 66

Howell, Evelyn (plant ecologist), 45–47, 70

Howett, Catherine, 67

Hudson, Henry, 124–25

Hunt, Tom, and Wazee Lake Park, 65, 171n17

IFLA. *See* International Federation of Landscape Architects

Iliad (Alexander), 97

imported species, 11

Indiana Dunes, 49

Institute of Ecology, University of Georgia, 84

interdisciplinarity, value of, 85, 92

International Federation of Landscape Architects, 110, 117

invasive species and weeds, control of, 99–101, 115, 131–32, 139–41, 148; and allelopathic species, 163

Iowa State College (now Iowa State University): landscape architecture curriculum, 21–24; Morrison at, 18–19, 21–24; Olmsted Brothers and, 21; O. C. Simonds and, 21; VEISHEA festival at, 19

IPHAN (National Institute of Historic and Artistic Heritage / Instituto do Patrimônio Histórico e Artístico Nacional, Brazil), 109

Jackson County Iron Company (WI), 64

Jensen, Jens: 48–51, 59, 170n6; on clients, 143; and council rings, 50, 56, 57; on curves in landscape design, 49; on birches, 49; and Fair Lane (Henry Ford estate, Dearborn, MI), 49, 93; and Friends of Our Native Landscape, 58, 170n14; Lincoln Memorial Garden (Springfield, IL), 93; and mass and space, 60; on music and landscape design, 57, 83; papers located, 58–59; and The Ridges Sanctuary, 54; and "sun openings," 50, 56; on trails, 53–54; and Frank Lloyd Wright, 50–51. *See also* Clearing, The; *Siftings*

Jens Jensen: Maker of Natural Parks and Gardens (Grese), 93

John R. Bracken Lecture and Bracken Medal, Pennsylvania State University, 101

Johnson, Clair and Dorothy, 50

Johnson, Lady Bird (Claudia Alta), 94–95; and highway beautification, 36; and National Wildflower Research Center, 87

Jones, Samuel (taxonomist), 70–71

Kalsow Prairie State Preserve (Iowa), *4, 10*

Kandinsky, Wassily, 121

Kansas City Art Institute, 18
Kaplan, Rachel, 85, 92–93
Kaplan, Stephen, 85
Kasakaitas, William, 58
Kellenberg (Mensing), Louise (aunt), 18
Kellenberg, Richard (landscape architect), 18
Kemple, Frank (landscape architect), 32, 34–35, 101
Kennedy, Jacqueline, 29, 35
Kennedy, John F., 29, 35
King, Martin Luther, Jr., 83
Kjelgren, Roger, 117–18
Kondis, Joseph (LA), 31–33, 35, 101, 169n1

Lancaster County, Nebraska, county plan project, 26
Landscape Architecture Magazine (formerly *Landscape Architecture Quarterly*), 25, 43, 61
Landscape Artist in America: The Life and Work of Jens Jensen (Eaton), 49–50
Landscape Journal, 65–66
"Landscape Luminosity" (Bye), 43–44
Landscaping on the New Frontier (Meyer, Kjelgren, Morrison, and Varga), 117–18
late-successional species. *See* successional species
LBJ Ranch (now Lyndon B. Johnson National Historical Park), 94–95
Lenni Lenapi people, 124
Leopold, Aldo, 170n1; and ecological restoration, 39; *Sand County Almanac,* 39–41, 65; and University of Wisconsin Arboretum, 39
Liberman, Alexander: *Iliad, 97, 98*
Lima, Catharina, 84
Lincoln, Nebraska, city plan project, 25–26
Lincoln Memorial Garden (Springfield, IL), 49, 93
Lindquist, Peter, 65
Lodde's Mill Bluff (WI), 107
Long, Gregory, 126–27, 130
longleaf pine savannas, *74, 75,* 75–77
Lorimer, Uli, 136–37, 139–40
Lovelace, Eldridge (landscape architect), 24–25, 169n3
"Love" movement, *Muir Woods Suite* (Duke), 83, 104–5
"Low" Symphony (Glass), 83
luminosity, concept of, 43–44, 136–37, 163

Lyndon B. Johnson National Historical Park. *See* LBJ Ranch

Mack Scogin Merrill Elam Architects, 144
Man and Pegasus (Milles), 18
Manassas National Battlefield Park, restoration project, 85–86
Mannahatta: A Natural History of New York City (Sanderson), 125–26
Manhattan, native plants of, 124–26
Martin Luther King Jr. Memorial, competition entry, 83
Maryland-National Capital Park and Planning Commission, Morrison at, 31, 35
mass:space concept and plans: defined, 35–36; Jensen and, 60; in nature, 117; at University of Wisconsin Arboretum, Native Plant Garden, 103–5, *104;* and use of music, 104–5
McCord, Bruce, 101–2, 114, 132
McCord, Kim, 102, 114
McKinney, Eleanor (landscape architect), 87
meadows, converting turf lawns and fields to, 99–102, 141, 144–45, *144, 146*
Mendelssohn, Felix, "Spring Song," 83
Mensing, Raymond (uncle), 18
Meyer, Susan, 117–18
mid-successional species. *See* successional species
Miller, Steve, and founding of *Landscape Journal,* 65–66
Milles, Carl, *Man and Pegasus,* 18
moisture continuum: dry, 44, 103, 106, *108,* 113, *114,* 165; in Hempstead Plains (Long Island), 137; mesic, *frontispiece, 40, 41, 42, 106, 110;* wet, 105; wet-mesic, *112*
Moldau, The (Smetana), 22, 84
Mon Père, Mon Père (di Suvero), *140*
Montana ranch project, 153–63, *159, 160;* balsamroot, 153–54, *155, 157;* council ring, 155–56, *156,* 163; "dot" drawings (planting plans), 159–60, 163; environment, 156–57; as evolving landscape, 163; guest house area, 153–54, *155, 157, 157,* 160–61; limber pines, 153–54, *157, 158, 160;* native landscape, *154;* paths and walkways, 154–55, *157,* 161, *162;* plants used, 156–57, *157,* 159–61, *160;* pond area, *161;* rivers

and drifts, 160; terraces, 153–54, 159
Morrison, Dawna Hauptman (wife), 31, 36–37, 66, 69
Morrison, Darrel, *8, 14, 16, 23, 54, 158, 167;* acting classes and roles, 82–83, 116, 122; art, interest in, 3, 18–19, 36, 121; Bracken Medal and lecture (Pennsylvania State University), 101; Brazil, travel to, 109–10, 115, 117; children, 36, 62, 66, 69–70, 81–83, 109–10, 119; Driftless Area property (Iowa County, WI; now Morrison Prairie & Forest Preserve), 113–15, *114,* 119, 167; early life, 3–5, 7–18; education, 18–19, 21–24, 36–37, 39–43; Madison (WI) apartment, 165; marriage, 31, 36–37, 66, 69; military service, 26–29; music, interest in, 18, 22, 56–57, 83; New York City visits and homes, 25–26, 82–83, 115–17, 119, 121, 165; Oconee River (GA) home, 79–81, *81,* 84, 121; running, 66; theater, interest in, 22, 25, 82–83, 121–22; watercolor sketches, *55, 88, 123. See also* design philosophy and concepts; projects; publications; teaching and administration
Morrison, Eldon (brother), 7, *8,* 15, *16, 18–19,* 69
Morrison, Jon (son), 36, 62, 66, 69, 110, 119
Morrison, Kenneth (brother), 7, *8,* 15, *16,* 18
Morrison, Lisa (niece), 69
Morrison, Raymond and Rosy (parents), 7, *8,* 11–15, 18–19, 69
Morrison, Scott (son), 66, 69–70, 81–83, 109, 119
Morrison farm (near Orient, IA), 3–5, 7, 11–17, *14, 16*
Morrison Prairie & Forest Preserve (WI), 167
Morton Arboretum (Lisle, IL), 51, 59
Mother Peace (di Suvero), *140*
"moving spaces." *See* mass:space concept and plans
Muir, John, 105
Muir Woods Suite (Duke), 83, 104–5
Municipal Opera Theatre (St. Louis), 25
music: in Designing with Music and other courses, 84, 89, 93; in design process, 57, 83–84, 93, 104–5; Jensen and, 57, 83
"My Heart at Thy Sweet Voice" (Saint-Saëns), 84

"mystery–complexity–coherence–legibility" concept, 85, 92

National Gallery (Washington, D.C.), 36
National Park Service, projects for, 85–86, 94, 171n1
National Wildflower Research Center: Designing for Place course taught at, 94; founding of, 86–87
National Wildflower Research Center headquarters project (Austin, TX), 86, 87, 86–88, 94; opening, 97
Native Americans: and *Beauty of the Wild* (Goodman), 56; and controlled burns 9, 63, 114–15; Lenni Lenapi people, 124; trails, 53–54
native plant communities, as a basis for design, 32; *American Plants for American Gardens* and, 32–33, 118; and Atlanta History Center project, 89, 92; and CUNA Mutual Insurance Company project, 60–61; and National Wildflower Research Center project, 87–88; Native Plant Communities of Wisconsin course, 44–47; Native Plant Communities of the Southeast course, 70–71, 89, 115, 117; and Round House project, 144, 146–46; and University of Wisconsin Arboretum, Native Plant Garden project, 102–3, 107; and *The Vegetation of Wisconsin* (Curtis), 42; and Walden Park project, 89; and Wheaton Youth Center project, 31–32
Native Woodland Garden in Schwartz Plaza: Plant Field Guide (Clark), 126
Nature Conservancy, The, 73, 79, 94
nature preserves, importance of, 77, 79
Nelson, Gaylord, 59
Neruda's Gate (di Suvero), *133*
"Nessun Dorma" (Puccini), 83
New Observatory Woods (WI), 107
New York Botanical Garden, Old Stone Mill site project, 126–32, *129, 130, 131;* plants used, 127–28, *128, 130, 131,* 132; "rivers and drifts" concept, 127–28, 130
New York Botanical Garden, School of Professional Horticulture, 122–23
New York University, Native Woodland Garden project, 124–26
Ninety Six National Historic Site (SC), consulting project, 94

Northington, David, 86–88
NWRC. *See* National Wildflower Research Center

Oconee River (GA), 79–81, *80;* Morrison's home on, 79–81, *81,* 84, 121
Odum, Eugene, 84–85, 92
Ogden, Ralph E., 98
Okefenokee Swamp (GA and FL), *78,* 78–79
Old Stone Mill. *See* New York Botanical Garden, Old Stone Mill site project
Olmsted Brothers firm: and Iowa State campus expansion, 21; and Rock Creek Parkway, 34–35
Overland Partners (architectural firm), 87

Pennsylvania State University, landscape architecture program, 32
Petersburg National Battlefield (VA), consulting project, 94
Piedmont. *See* Georgia Piedmont region
pine barrens: in Brooklyn Botanic Garden, Native Flora Garden Extension project, *135,* 135–39, *137,* 140–41; Long Island, 136; lowland, 137–38; New Jersey, 118, 136–37, 139; upland, *135,* 137–38, *138,* 140
Pinelands National Reserve (NJ), 118
Pinelands Preservation Alliance, 136
Pollack, Jackson, and jazz, 84
"pollinator" gardens, 55
prairies, types of: dry, 44, 103, 106, *108,* 113, *114,* 165; mesic, *frontispiece, 40, 41, 42,* 106, *110;* tallgrass (*see* tallgrass prairies); wet, 105; wet-mesic, *112. See also* grasslands, eastern U.S.
projects: Atlanta History Center, museum building and granite outcrop garden, 89–92, *90, 91;* Bayfield, WI, design and planning guidelines for, 36–37; Brooklyn Botanic Garden, Native Flora Garden Extension, 134–41, *135, 137, 138;* CUNA Mutual Insurance Company headquarters (Madison, WI), 60–61, 93–94; at District of Columbia Department of Highways and Traffic, 36; General Electric Medical Systems Division (Pewaukee, WI), *61, 62,* 61–63; at Harland Bartholomew & Associates (St. Louis), 24–26; Jackson County Iron Company tailings

basin, 64–65; Manassas National Battlefield Park restoration, 85–86; Martin Luther King Jr. Memorial competition entry, 83; at Maryland-National Capital Park and Planning Commission, 31–35; Montana ranch, 153–63, *154, 155, 156, 157, 158, 159, 160, 161, 162;* national battlefield and military parks, 85–86, 94; National Wildflower Research Center headquarters, *86, 87,* 86–88, 94; New York Botanical Garden, Old Stone Mill site design, 126–32, *128, 129, 130, 131;* New York University, Native Woodland Garden, 124–26; Rock Creek Parkway (Montgomery County, MD), planting plan, 34; Round House (Wilton, CT), 143–51, *144, 146, 147, 148, 149, 150, 151;* Storm King Art Center (near Cornwall, NY), 97–102, 114–16, *116,* 132–34, *133, 134, 140,* 141; at Thurman Donovan & Associates, 35–36; University of Wisconsin Arboretum, Native Plant Garden, *6, 42,* 102–9, *103, 104, 107, 109, 110, 111, 112,* 139; Utah State University Botanical Center, design and planning for, 117–18; Walden Park (Madison, WI), 59–61, *60. See also individual project entries*
"prospect-refuge" theory, 84, 155
publications: *American Plants for American Gardens,* foreword to reprint edition, 101; in *Guide to Sustainable Earthworks Management* (NPS), 94, 171n1; *Landscape Journal,* founding editor of, 65–66; in *Landscaping on the New Frontier* (Meyer, Kjelgren, Morrison, and Varga), 117–18; "Research: Vegetation and Iron Ore Tailings," 171n16; "Restoring the Midwestern Landscape," 61
Puccini, Giacomo, "Nessun Dorma," 83
Pyramidian (di Suvero), *99, 140*

quadrats (vegetation sampling plots) and line transects, 45–47, 92

Rehmann, Elsa, 32–33, 70, 101, 118, 169–70n3. See also *American Plants for American Gardens*
Reis, George, 124–26

"Restoring the Midwestern Landscape" (Morrison), 61
Rice, Thomas (stonemason), 90, 92
Richmond National Battlefield Park (VA), consulting project, 94
Ridges Sanctuary, The (Bailey's Harbor, WI), 54
Risk, Kevin (preservationist), 94
"rivers and drifts" concept: at Montana ranch project, 160; at New York Botanical Garden, Old Stone Mill project, 127–28, 130; at Storm King, 99
Roberto Burle Marx: um retrato (Fleming), 110
Roberts, Edith, 32–33, 49, 70, 101, 169–70n3. See also *American Plants for American Gardens*
Roberts Edith, and Elsa Rehmann, *American Plants for American Gardens,* 32–33, *34,* 35–36, 70, 118, 169–70n3; reprint with Morrison foreword (1996), 101
Rock Creek Parkway project, planting plan, 34–35
Roosevelt, Franklin Delano, 78–79
Roosevelt, Theodore, 79
Rothacker, Ralph R. (Iowa State professor), 19, 24; and Iowa State College campus expansion, 21
Round House project (Wilton, CT), 143–51, *147, 149, 151;* aspen–sumac grove, 145; eastern parcel (2016), 145–46; as evolving ecosystem, 149–51; lawn to meadow conversion, 144–45, *144, 146;* and native cultivars, 146–48; original house design and remodel, 143–44; plants used, 145–48, *146, 148, 150;* pond area, 144–45, 148; rock garden, 145; weed control, 148
Rust, Maude, 19
Rutgers University, teaching at, 118, 121
Rutherford, William A., Sr. (landscape architect), 97

Saarinen, Eliel, 18
Saint-Saëns, Camille, "My Heart at Thy Sweet Voice," 84
saltmarshes, 76, 77–78
Sand County Almanac (Leopold), 39–41, 65, 170n.1
Sanderson, Eric W., *Mannahatta: A Natural History of New York City,* 125–26

savannas: black oak and bur oak in Native Plant Garden, University of Wisconsin Arboretum, *41,* 105, *109, 111;* at Brooklyn Botanic Garden, Native Flora Garden Extension, 135–36; longleaf pine, *74, 75*
Schleiter, Kristin, 129
Schooner Cove, Acadia National Park, *33*
Schuler, Jessica, 132
Schunnemunk Fork (Serra), *101*
Schwartz, Martha (landscape architect), 93
Schwartz Plaza. *See* New York University, Native Woodland Garden project
Seaman, Mike, 133
seed collecting, 59, 62–63, 65, 136, 139
Serra, Richard, *Schunnemunk Fork, 101*
Shemwell, Robert (architect), 87
Shrubs and Vines for American Gardens (Wyman), 24, 32
Siftings (Jensen), 49; on birches, 49; on clients, 143; on council rings, 50; on curves, 49; on music and landscape design, 57, 83; on trails, 53–54
Simonds, Ossian Cole (landscape architect), 93, 169n6; and Iowa State College campus design, 21
Simonds, Robert Cole (city planner), 26, 169n6
SiteWorks (landscape architecture firm), 136, 138–39
Smetana, Bedřich, *The Moldau,* 22, 84
Snelson, Kenneth, *Free Ride Home,* 98
Sotillo, James, 139
Southern Wildlands habitat preserves (IA), 9
"Spring Song" (Mendelssohn), 83
Stern, H. Peter, 98
Steven Dubner Landscaping, 139
Stones River National Battlefield (TN), consulting project, 94
Storm King Art Center project (near Cornwall, NY), 97–100, *98,* 114–15, 132–34; controlled burns, 114–15, 133, 141; cover crops, 99–102; as evolving landscape, 141; gravel quarry area plantings, 132–34, *133;* origin, 98; plants used, 99–100, *100,* 102, 115, *116, 132*–34, *134;* "rivers and drifts" concept, 99; setting and sculptures, 97–98, *97, 98, 99, 100, 101,* 102, *116, 140,* 141; tallgrass plantings, *100, 101,* 114–16, *133, 134, 140;* weed control, 99–101, 115
Storm King Wall (Goldsworthy), *100*

Stovall, Allen, 67
Streeter, Tal, *Endless Column,* 98, 102
successional species: forbs, *63;* grasses, 64–65; natural process of, 41; trees, 52, 59, 89, 130–32, 146; wildflowers, *146*
Sundback, Eric, 170n7; and mass:space plans, 35–36
Svenson, Henry K., 135
swamps: in Brooklyn Botanic Garden, Native Flora Garden Extension, 137–38; Okefenokee (GA and FL), *78,* 78–79
Swink, Floyd, 51–52, 55, 170n11

tallgrass prairies: controlled burns in, 9, 63–64; as farmland, 10–11; imported species, 10–11; native species, *frontispiece, 2, 4,* 9–11, *13, 20, 30, 39, 44, 68, 96, 165, 166;* natural fires in, 9; original extent and character of, 7–10; preserves, *4, 9, 10, 12, 13, 46,* 167 (*see also* University of Wisconsin Arboretum); similarity to eastern grasslands, 97, 136; trees, 9–10
Taylor, Norman, 134–35; *Botany: The Science of Plant Life,* 135
teaching and administration: at Black Rock Forest (NY), 122–24; at The Clearing, 54–56; at Columbia University, Master of Landscape Design program, 122; at Conway School of Landscape Design, 93–94; Designing for Place course (NWRC), 94; Designing with Music course (University of São Paulo), 84; and experience as actor, 83; for IFLA (Brazil), 117; music, use of, 83–84, 89, 93; at National Wildflower Research Center, 94; Native Plant Communities of Wisconsin course (University of Wisconsin), 44–47, 67; Native Plant Communities of the Southeast course (University of Georgia), 70–71, 89, 115, 117; at New York Botanical Garden, School of Professional Horticulture, 122–23; planting design courses, 43–44, 50, 59, 70, 83, 117–18, 122; at Rutgers University, 118, 121; at University of Georgia, School of Environmental Design (professor and dean), 66–67, 69–72, 78–79, 83–85, 89,

115, 117; at University of Michigan, School of Natural Resources and Environment, 92–93; at University of São Paulo, 110; at University of Wisconsin, 43–48, 59, 66, 102, 165–67; at Utah State University, 117–18

Teardrop Park (New York City), 117

Telfer, Sid and Inez, 50

Texas, native landscape of, *27*, 27–28, 94–95

Thurman Donovan & Associates, Morrison at, 35–36, 170n6

Tishler, William, 36–37; and Jensen, 48

Toft, Emma, 50, 54

Toft Point State Natural Area (Bailey's Harbor, WI), 54–55, *54, 55*

topographic base maps, 23

Town & Gown Players (Athens, GA), 82

transects and quadrats (vegetation sampling plots), 45–47, 92

Trees for American Gardens (Wyman), 24

Tropical Gardens of Burle Marx, The (Bardi), 42–43, 85

University of Georgia, Institute of Ecology, 84

University of Georgia, School of Environmental Design, Morrison at, 66–67, 69–72, 78–79, 83–85, 89, 115, 117

University of Georgia Press, 101

University of Michigan, Nichols Arboretum, 92

Untitled (von Schlegell), *116*

Utah State University, Botanical Center, design and planning for, 117–18``

Utah, native landscape of, 117–18

University of Wisconsin (Madison): arboretum (*see* University of Wisconsin Arboretum); CELA annual meeting at (1981), 65; Kemp Natural Resources Station, 45, 47;

landscape architecture program, 36, 43; Morrison at (MA program), 36–37, 39–43; Morrison's teaching at, 43–48, 59, 66, 165–67; Jon Morrison at, 69; and Walden Park project, 59–60; Zoe Bayliss Women's Cooperative dormitory, 59

University of Wisconsin Arboretum: Curtis Prairie, 39–41, *40*, 102, *105, 106;* Greene Prairie, *40;* as early ecological restoration, 39, *40,* 59, 93, 102, 109; founding of, 39; Leopold and, 39; and teaching, 43–44; visitor center, 102, 106. *See also* University of Wisconsin Arboretum, Native Plant Garden project

University of Wisconsin Arboretum, Native Plant Garden project, 102–9, *103,* 167; Black Oak and Bur Oak Savanna sections, *41,* 105, *109, 111;* Susan Carpenter and, 109, 167; dominant, abundant, and "visual essence" species representations, 102, 139; forest sections (maple-basswood, oak-hickory, cedar-birch), *41,* 105, *107;* grading and soil modification, 103, 105–6; Limestone Prairie section, 106, *108;* mass:space conceptual plan, 103–5, *104;* mesic prairie section, *frontispiece,* 40, *41, 42, 105, 106, 110;* plants used, 102–3, 105–7, *107, 110, 112, 113,* 139; Sand Prairie section, 102–3, 106; site, 102–3; vegetation zones, 103–5; "vignettes," 102, *114;* visitor center area, 105–6; wet-mesic prairie section, *112;* wetlands, *41,* 105, *113*

Utah, native landscape of, 117–18

Van Gogh, Vincent, 3; *Wheatfield under Thunderclouds* (1890), 3

Van Gogh Museum (Amsterdam), 3

Van Valkenburgh, Michael (landscape architect), 116–17

Varga, William, 117–18

Vegetation of the New Jersey Pine-Barrens, The (Harshberger), 136–37

Vegetation of Wisconsin, The (Curtis), 41–42, 102

vegetation sampling, 39, 94; quadrats and transects in, 45–47, 92

VEISHEA festival (Iowa State College), 19

Vilas Running Club, 66

"visual essence," 47, 55, 88–89, 92; species, 102, 139

von Schlegell, David, *Untitled, 116*

Walden Park project (Madison, WI), 59–61, *60*

Walker, Donald, 93–94

Waterman Prairie Wildlife Management Area (IA), 12

Watson, Clair, 22

Wazee Lake Park (Jackson County, WI), 65

"Wedding Day at Troldhaugen" (Grieg), 56

weed control. *See* invasive species and weeds, control of

Westmacott, Richard, 67

Wilkus, Annette, 136

windbreaks, on midwestern prairie farms, 3, 7

Wolf, Marc, 129, 139

Wright, Frank Lloyd, and Jensen, 50–51

Wright, George, 81, 84

Wyman, Donald: *Shrubs and Vines for American Gardens,* 24, 32; *Trees for American Gardens,* 24

Yurgalevitch, Charles, 122

Ziegler, George (landscape architect), 48–49

98: Alexander Liberman. *Adam*, 1970. Painted steel, 28 ft. 6 in. x 24 ft. x 29 ft. 6 in. (868.7 x 731.5 x 899.2 cm). Gift of the Ralph E. Ogden Foundation. © The Alexander Liberman Trust. Photo by Jerry L. Thompson. Courtesy Storm King Art Center, Mountainville, NY.

99: Mark di Suvero. *Pyramidian*, 1987/1998. Steel, 65 x 46 x 46 ft. (19.8 x 14 x 14 m). Gift of the Ralph E. Ogden Foundation. *Beethoven's Quartet*, 2003. Steel, stainless steel, 24 ft. 7 in. x 30 in. x 23 ft. 3 in. (749.3 x 76.2 x 708.7 cm). Courtesy Tippet Rise Art Center. © Mark di Suvero, courtesy the artist and Spacetime C.C., New York. Photo by Jerry L. Thompson. Courtesy Storm King Art Center, Mountainville, NY.

100: Andy Goldsworthy. *Storm King Wall*, 1997–98. Fieldstone, 60 in. x 2278 ft. 6 in. x 32 in. (152.4 cm x 694.5 m x 81.3 cm). Gift of the Ralph E. Ogden Foundation, Mr. and Mrs. Joel Mallin, Mrs. W. L. Lyons Brown, Jr., Mr. and Mrs. James H. Ottaway, Jr., the Margaret T. Morris Foundation, The Horace W. Goldsmith Foundation, the Hazen Fund, the Joseph H. Hazen Foundation, Inc., Mr. and Mrs. Ronald N. Romary, Dr. Wendy Schaffer and Mr. Ivan Gjaja, and an anonymous foundation. © Andy Goldsworthy, courtesy Galerie Lelong & Co., New York. Photo by Jerry L. Thompson. Courtesy Storm King Art Center, Mountainville, NY.

101: Richard Serra. *Schunnemunk Fork*, 1990–91. Weathering steel. 8 ft. x 49 ft. 1 in. x 2½ in. (243.8 cm x 15 m x 6.3 cm). 8 ft. x 35 ft. 1 in. x 2½ in. (243.8 cm x 10.7 m x 6.3 cm). 8 ft. x 38 ft. 4 in. x 2½ in. (243.8 cm x 11.7 m x 6.3 cm). 8 ft. x 54 ft. 4 in. x 2½ in. (243.8 cm x 16.6 m x 6.3 cm). Gift of the Ralph E. Ogden Foundation by exchange, The Brown Foundation, Inc., and an anonymous foundation. © 2020 Richard Serra/Artists Rights Society (ARS), New York. Photo by Jerry L. Thompson. Courtesy Storm King Art Center, Mountainville, NY.

116: David von Schlegell. *Untitled*, 1972. Aluminum and stainless steel. 20 ft. x 25 ft. 4 in. x 16 ft. (609.6 x 772.2 x 487.7 cm). Purchased with the aid of funds from the National Endowment for the Arts and gift of the Ralph E. Ogden Foundation. Photo by Jerry L. Thompson. Courtesy Storm King Art Center, Mountainville, NY.

133: Chakaia Booker. *Foci*, 2010. Rubber tire and stainless steel. 30 x 8 x 8 ft. (914.4 x 243.8 x 243.8 cm). Courtesy the artist. Mark di Suvero. *Neruda's Gate*, 2005. Steel. 26 ft. 9 ⅝ in. x 25 ft. x 8 ft. (816.9 x 762 x 243.8 cm). Lent by the artist and Spacetime C.C., New York. © Mark di Suvero, courtesy of the artist and Spacetime C.C., New York. Photo by Jerry L. Thompson. Courtesy Storm King Art Center, Mountainville, NY.

140: View of the South Fields, all works by Mark di Suvero. Except where noted, all works gift of the Ralph E. Ogden Foundation. Background: *Pyramidian*, 1987/1998. Steel, 65 x 46 x 46 ft. (19.8 x 14 x 14 m). *Beethoven's Quartet*, 2003. Steel, stainless steel, 24 ft. 7 in. x 30 in. x 23 ft. 3 in. (749.3 x 76.2 x 708.7 cm). Courtesy Tippet Rise Art Center. *Mon Père, Mon Père*, 1973–75. Steel. 35 ft. x 40 ft. x 40 ft. 4 in. (10.7 x 12.2 x 12.3 m). *Mother Peace*, 1969–70. Painted steel. 41 ft. 8 in. x 49 ft. 5 in. x 44 ft. 3 in. (12.7 x 15.1 x 13.5 m). © Mark di Suvero, courtesy the artist and Spacetime C.C., New York. Photo by Jerry L. Thompson. Courtesy Storm King Art Center, Mountainville, NY.